Lawrie Ryan

Top Chemistry Grades for You

GCSE Revision Guide for AQA Modular

Contents

To see the latest Exam Specification for AQA Modular Science, visit **www.aqa.org.uk**

To see this Exam Specification 'mapped' with the relevant pages in ***Chemistry for You***, visit **www.chemistryforyou.co.uk**

Introduction

Top Chemistry Grades for You is designed to help you achieve the best possible grades in your GCSE examination.

It focuses on exactly what you need to do to succeed in the AQA Modular Science exam (for Single or for Double Award, and at either Foundation or Higher Tier), or in the AQA Modular Chemistry exam.

There is a separate book for AQA Coordinated Science and AQA Chemistry B.

This revision book is best used together with the ***Chemistry for You*** textbook, but it can also be used by itself.

There are also books for
Top Biology Grades for You and
Top Physics Grades for You.

For each section in the AQA Modular Science examination specification, there is a Topic as shown on the opposite page.

For each Topic there are 2 double-page spreads:

- a **Revision** spread, which shows you exactly what you need to know (see below), and
- a **Questions** spread, which lets you try out some exam questions on this topic.
  The **Answers** for these, with Examiners' Tips, are given at the back of the book.

In addition, for each section of Topics there is:

- a **Sample Answer** spread, showing you answers at Grade-A level and at Grade-C level, with Examiners' Comments and Tips. These will help you to focus on how to improve, to move up to a higher grade.

Each Revision spread is laid out clearly, using boxes:

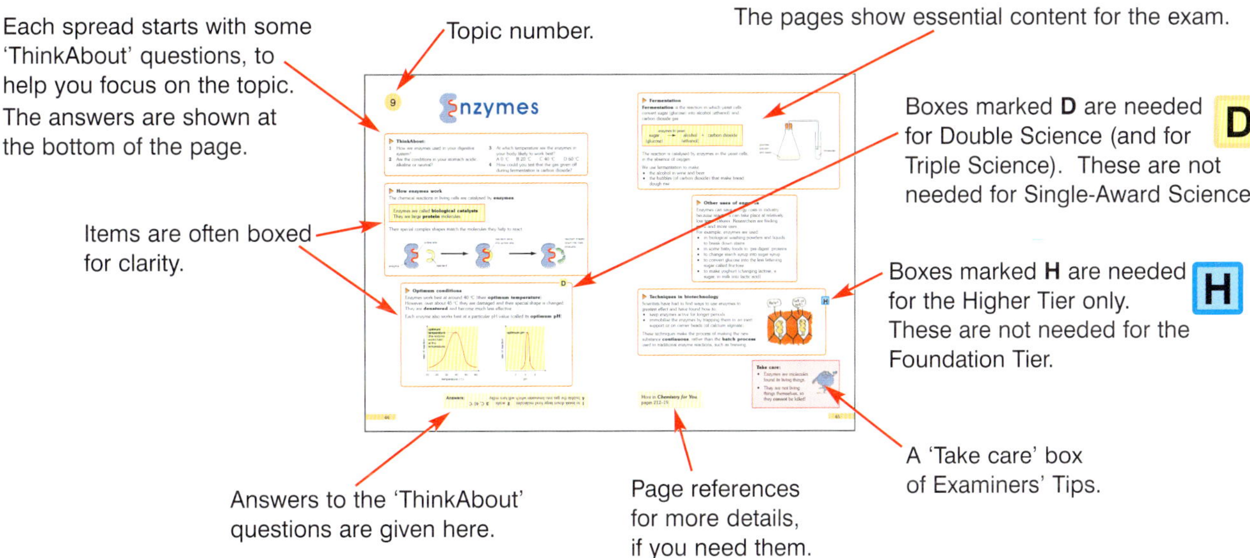

As a first step, go through this book and:

- If you are studying for Single-Award Science, cross out all the boxes labelled **D**
- If you are studying for the Foundation Tier, cross out all the boxes labelled **H**
- If you are **not** studying for Triple Award Chemistry, cross out all of Topics 19, 20, 21, 22 and 23.

Then use the pull-out **Revision Calendar** to keep a record of your progress.

At the back of the book there are detachable **Revision Cards**, with very brief summaries. You can use these to top up your revision in spare moments – for example, when sitting on a bus or waiting for a lesson.

Best wishes for a great result in your exams.

Lawrie Ryan

Revision Technique

Prepare

1. Go through the book, crossing out any boxes that you don't need (as described at the bottom of page 3).
2. While doing this, you can decide which are your strong topics, and which topics you need to spend more time on.
3. You need to balance your time between:
   - **Revising** what you need to know about Chemistry. To do this, use the first double-page spread in each topic.
   - **Practising** by doing exam questions. To do this, use the second spread in each topic.

   Do these two things for each topic in turn.

Revise

4. Think about your best ways of revising. Some of the best ways are to do something ***active***. To use active learning you can:
   - Write down **notes**, as a summary of the topic (while reading through the double-page spread). Use highlighter pens to colour key words.
   - Make a **poster** to summarise each topic (and pin it up on your bedroom wall?). Make it colourful, and use images/sketches if you can.
   - Make a spider-diagram or **mind map** of each topic. See the example here, but use your own style:
   - Ask someone (family or friend) to **test** you on the topic.
   - **Teach** the topic to someone (family or friend).

   Which method works best for you?
5. It is usually best to work in a quiet room, for about 25–30 minutes at a time, and then take a 5–10 minute break.
6. After you have revised a topic, make a note of the date on the pull-out **Revision Calendar**.

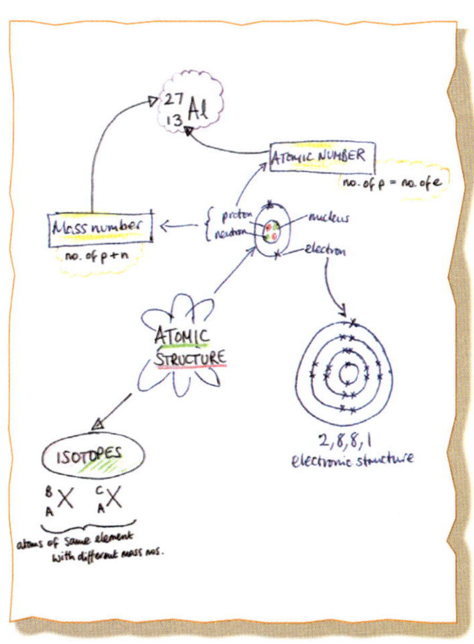

*A **Mind Map** for Topic 14: Atomic Structure.*

*A Mind Map always makes more sense when you make it **yourself**.*

Use colour and images if you can.

Practise

7. When you have revised a topic, and think you know it well, then it's important to practise it, by answering some exam questions. Turn to the second spread of the topic and answer the questions as well as you can.
8. When you have finished them, turn to the **Answers and Examiners' Tips** that start on page 108. Check your answers, and read the Examiners' Hints. Can you see how to improve your answers in future?
9. Keep a record of your progress on the **Revision Calendar**.

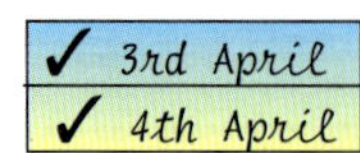

Re-revise and Top-up

10. It is important to re-revise each topic again, after an interval. The best intervals are after 10 minutes, after 1 day, and after 1 week (see the graphs in ***Chemistry for You***, pages 384–385).

    For this top-up you can use the topic spread, your notes, poster or mindmap, and the **Revision Cards** at the back of this book.

A revision flowchart:

Choose a topic to revise.

1. Revise

- **ThinkAbout** : try the questions in the ThinkAbout box. The answers are at the bottom of the page.
- **Read** the rest of the double-page spread. Focus on any parts you are not sure about.
- **Do** make Notes, or a Poster, or a Mind Map. Highlight key points in colour.
- **Re-read** the spread after a break of 5–10 minutes.
- **Take care** : read the 'Take care' box. Can you see how you can use this advice?
- ✓ **Tick and date** the pull-out Revision Calendar.

2. Practise

- **Try** the questions on the double-page of questions. These are in the same style as the ones in the exam.
- **Check** your answers. The answers begin on page 108. Read the Examiners' Hints carefully. Go back over anything you find difficult.
- ✓ **Tick and date** the pull-out Revision Calendar to keep a record of your progress.

Then later:

Re-visit
Re-visit each topic 1 day later, and then 1 week later.
Read the double-page spread, your notes or Mind Map, and the questions you answered.

Up your Grade
At the end of each section of topics, read the Sample Answers at Grade A and Grade C.
Look at the Hints and Tips for improving your grade.

Top-up
Use the Revision Cards to remind you of the key points, and test yourself.
Even better, make your own Revision Cards.

Examination Technique

Before the exam

1. Make sure you know the dates and times of all your exams, so that you are not late!
   See the table at the bottom of this page.
2. Make sure you know which topics are going to be examined on which paper.
3. On the night before the exam, it may help to do some quick revision – but don't do too much.
   Make sure you get a good night's sleep.

On the day of the exam

1. Aim to arrive early at the exam room.
2. Make sure that you are properly equipped with pens and pencils (including spares), a rubber, a ruler, a calculator (check the battery!) and a watch.

During the exam

1. Don't waste time when you get the paper. Write your name and candidate number (unless they are already printed).
   Read the instructions on the front page of the booklet, carefully, and make sure you follow them.
2. Read each question very carefully.
   In each question there is always a 'command' word that tells you what to do.
   If the question says '***State ...***' or '***List ...***' or '***Name ...***' then you should give a short answer.
   If the question says '***Explain ...***' or '***Describe ...***' or '***Why does ...***' or '***Suggest ...***' then you should make sure you give a longer answer.

   Put a ring round each 'command' word.

   Then underline the key words in the question.
   For example:

   > Describe in detail what you would see when a small piece of sodium is placed in a trough of cold water.

   Then you can see exactly what is given to you in the question, and what you have to do.

   Make sure that you answer only the question shown on the exam paper (not the one that you wish had been asked).

One way of collecting information about all your exams (in all your subjects):

Date, time and room	**Subject, paper number and tier**	**Length (hours)**	**Types of question:** **– structured?** **– single word answers?** **– longer answers?** **– essays?**	**Sections?**	**Details of choice (if any)**	**Approximate time per mark (minutes)**
5th June 9.30 Hall	Science (Double Award) Paper 2 (Chemistry) Higher Tier	$1\frac{1}{2}$	Structured questions (with single-word answers and longer answers)	1	no choice	1 min.

Answering the questions

Structured questions

- Make sure you know exactly what the question is asking.
- Look for the number of marks awarded for each part of the question. For example *(2 marks)* means that the Examiner will expect 2 main (and different) points in your answer.
- The number of lines of space is also a guide to how much you are expected to write.
- Make sure that you use any data provided in the question.
- Pace yourself with a watch so that you don't run out of time. You should aim to use 1 minute for each mark. So if a question has 3 marks it should take you about 3 minutes.
- In calculations, show all the steps in your working. This way you may get marks for the way you tackle the problem, even if your final answer is wrong. Make sure that you put the correct units in the answer.
- Try to write something for each part of every question.
- Follow the instructions given in the question. If it asks for one answer, give only one answer.
- If you have spare time at the end, use it wisely.

Extended questions

- Some questions require longer answers, where you will need to write two or more full sentences.
- The questions may include the words '***Describe***...' or '***Explain***...' or '***Evaluate***...' or '***Suggest***...' or '***Why does***...'.
- Make sure that the sentences are in good English and are linked to each other.
- Make sure you use scientific words in your answer.
- As before, the marks and the number of lines will give you a guide of how much to write. Make sure you include enough detail with at least as many points as there are marks.
- For the highest grades you need to include full details, in scientific language, written in good English, and with the sentences linking together in the correct sequence.

For multiple-choice questions:

- Read the instructions carefully.
- Mark the answer sheet exactly as you are instructed.
- If you have to rub out an answer, make sure that you rub it out well, so no pencil mark is left.
- Even if the answer looks obvious, look at all the alternatives before making a decision.
- If you are not sure of the answer, then first delete any answers that look wrong.
- If you still don't know the answer, then make an educated guess!
- Make sure that you give an answer to every question.

1 Metals in The Periodic Table

ThinkAbout:

1 Name the metals with the following chemical symbols:
a) Zn b) Li c) Fe d) Cr

2 Give the chemical symbols for the following metals:
a) sodium b) potassium c) copper

The Periodic Table

Each colour shows a chemical family of similar elements.

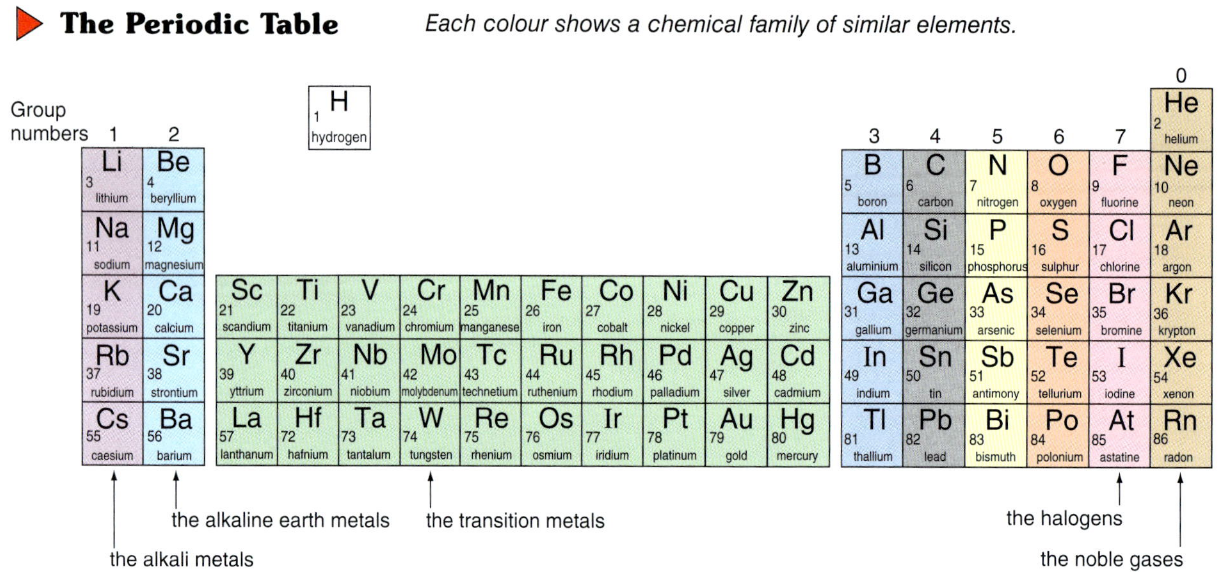

Look at the Periodic Table above:
We can arrange the chemical elements in order of their relative atomic masses.
Similar elements are lined up in columns called **groups**.
Each new row is called a **period**, starting with H and He in the first period.

Sometimes two elements don't line up in the right group, so this order has to change e.g. argon and potassium. You can see why this happens on page 74.

Metals make up over three-quarters of all the elements.
In the Periodic Table, they are found in Groups 1 and 2, the central block and sometimes in the right-hand block.

The alkali metals

The **Group 1** metals are called the **alkali metals**. **D**

For metals, they have low densities and are soft.
They are very reactive metals.

They get more reactive as we go down the group. Their melting points decrease going down the group.

Most of the compounds of alkali metals are white and are soluble in water.

Answers: **1** a) zinc b) lithium c) iron d) chromium **2** a) Na b) K c) Cu

D

▶ The transition metals

In the central block of the Periodic Table we find the **transition metals**. These have the typical properties of metals.

They usually:

- have high melting points
- are good conductors of heat
- are good conductors of electricity
- can be hammered into shapes (are malleable)
- can be drawn out into wires (are ductile).

Transition metals are strong, tough and hard.

Transition metals are strong.

D

▶ Reactions of transition metals

The transition metals are **not very reactive**. However, some do corrode slowly in air (oxygen) and water.

They form **coloured compounds**. This has led to their use in pottery glazes.

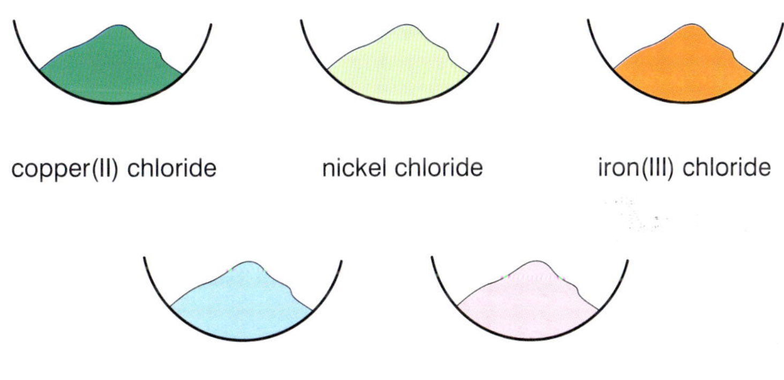

Transition metals are also important **catalysts** in industry. (Catalysts make reactions go faster. They remain chemically unchanged themselves at the end of the reaction. (See page 41.))

For example, iron is used in the making of ammonia. (See page 52.) Platinum is one of the catalysts used to make nitric acid. (See page 53.) It is also used in catalytic converters in car exhausts.

More in ***Chemistry for You***, pages 42–61.

Examination Questions – Metals in the Periodic Table

Year 10 questions

1 This question is about metals.
Match words from the list with each of the numbers **1–4** in the table.

iron
magnesium
mercury
potassium

Metal	What we can say about the metal
1	it is a transition metal, liquid at 20°C
2	it is extracted from the ore, haematite
3	it is used in alloys to make aluminium stronger
4	it reacts instantly with water to produce hydrogen

2 This passage is about the properties of some metals.
Match the words from the list with each of the spaces **1–4** in the passage.

conduct
corrode
cut
melt

Both alkali and transition metals ...... **1** ...... electricity well.

Because they are hard, transition metals do not ...... **2** .... as easily as alkali metals.

Transition metals react less quickly than alkali metals with water and oxygen so ....**3**...... more slowly.

Alkali metals ....**4**....... at a much lower temperature than transition metals.

3 The diagram shows an electrical cable.

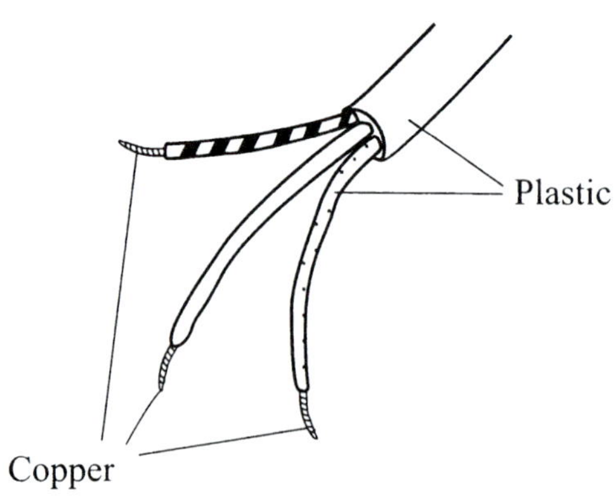

Which **two** of the following properties of copper make it suitable for the wire in the cables?

it bends and shapes easily
it does not react with dilute hydrochloric acid
it is a fairly expensive metal
it is a good conductor of electricity
it is a good conductor of heat

Year 11 questions

(You need to have covered Topics 14 and 16 to answer this question.)

1 The table shows part of a periodic table produced by a Russian chemist called Mendeleev in 1869.

Groups

1	2	3	4	5	6	7
H Hydrogen 1						
Li Lithium 7	Be Beryllium 9	B Boron 11	C Carbon 12	N Nitrogen 14	O Oxygen 16	F Fluorine 19
Na Sodium 23	Mg Magnesium 24	Al Aluminium 27	Si Silicon 28	P Phosphorus 31	S Sulphur 32	Cl Chlorine 35
K Potassium 39	Ca Calcium 40					

Marks

a) In what order did Mendeleev arrange the elements in his periodic table?

....

(1 mark)

b) Why did Mendeleev place beryllium, magnesium and calcium in the same Group?

....

....

(1 mark)

Look at the periodic table on the Data Sheet (see page 118) to answer the questions.

c) i In what order are the elements arranged in the periodic table shown on the Data Sheet?

....

(1 mark)

ii Look on the Data Sheet at the period (row) that begins with sodium and ends with argon.
Describe what happens to the number of electrons in the atoms in this period.

....

....

....

....

(2 marks) 5

2 Useful products from METAL ORES

ThinkAbout:

1. Name a metal that is less reactive than copper.
2. Which metal is used to make cooking foil?
3. Which metal is used to make electrical wires in household appliances?
4. Why are iron gates usually painted?
5. What do we call it when a compound is broken down by electricity?

The Reactivity Series

Metals can be put into order of reactivity in the **Reactivity Series**.

The metals higher up the Reactivity Series can **displace** those lower down from their compounds. For example:

magnesium + copper sulphate ⟶ magnesium sulphate + copper

$Mg + CuSO_4 \longrightarrow MgSO_4 + Cu$

Metals are found in the Earth's crust as metals themselves (for example, gold) or as metal compounds.

Ores are rocks that contain enough metal or its compound to make it economic to extract the metal.

We can predict how to extract a metal from its position in the Reactivity Series.

The highly reactive metals are difficult to extract.

We use electrolysis to extract these metals, such as sodium or aluminium.
The metals of medium reactivity can be extracted by reduction of the oxides with carbon.

potassium
sodium
magnesium
aluminium

carbon cannot be used to extract the more reactive metals

CARBON

zinc
iron
tin
lead
copper

these metals can be extracted using carbon

The blast furnace

We extract iron in a giant **blast furnace**.

1. The coke (carbon) reacts with oxygen in the hot air to make carbon dioxide.
   $C(s) + O_2(g) \longrightarrow CO_2(g)$
2. This carbon dioxide reacts with more hot coke to make **carbon monoxide** gas.
   $CO_2(g) + C(s) \longrightarrow 2\,CO(g)$
3. The carbon monoxide then **reduces** the iron oxide to iron.
   $Fe_2O_3(s) + 3\,CO(g) \longrightarrow 2\,Fe(l) + 3\,CO_2(g)$
4. Limestone gets rid of the sandy bits (acidic impurities) in the iron ore. They form a liquid **slag**.

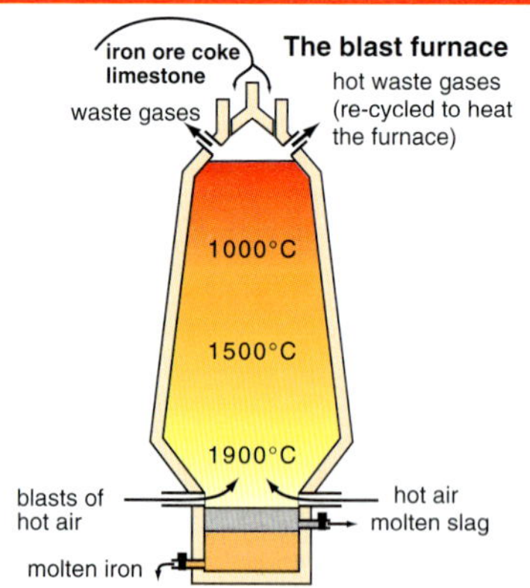

The iron from a blast furnace goes on to make **steel** (which usually contains over 95% iron). We have to protect the iron in steel from rusting. We can stop air and water getting to the iron by forming a barrier, for example by coating it with paint, plastic or tin.

However, it is more effective to attach a more reactive metal than iron (such as zinc or magnesium). The more reactive metal reacts in preference to iron and so protects it from rusting. This is called **sacrificial protection**. We can also add a little nickel or chromium in the steel-making process to form stainless steel (used for cutlery).

Answers: 1 silver/gold/platinum 2 aluminium 3 copper 4 to stop them rusting 5 electrolysis

 **Electrolysis** is the breakdown of a substance by electricity.

D

It is used to extract reactive metals, such as **aluminium**. Aluminium is found in its ore **bauxite**, which contains aluminium oxide.
The aluminium oxide is dissolved in molten cryolite. This lowers the melting point of aluminium oxide.

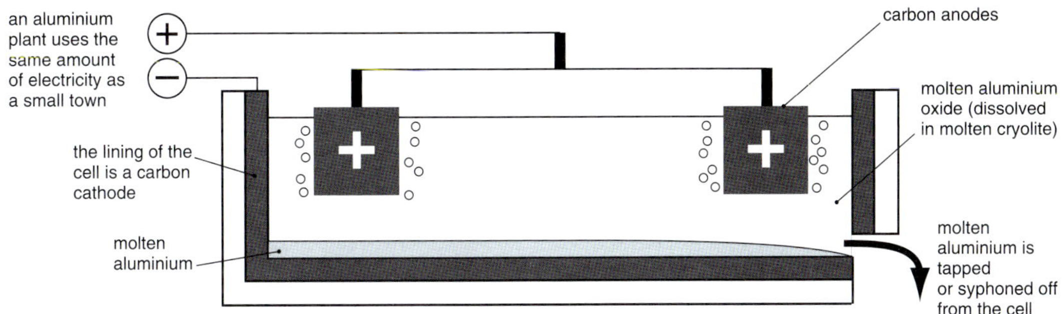

The electrodes are made of carbon.
Aluminium forms at the **cathode (−)**.
Carbon dioxide is given off from the **anode (+)**.
(The oxygen from the aluminium oxide reacts with the carbon anode to make carbon dioxide, so the anode gets burned away and has to be replaced frequently.)

The aluminium made is a very useful metal.
It resists corrosion because it is covered in a tough layer of aluminium oxide.
We can make it stronger by forming **alloys** by mixing in small amounts of other metals, such as magnesium.
These alloys are much harder and stiffer than pure aluminium.

D

Copper is **purified** by electrolysis.

The anode is the impure copper. The cathode is pure copper.

The copper electrodes dip into a solution containing copper ions which are positively charged.

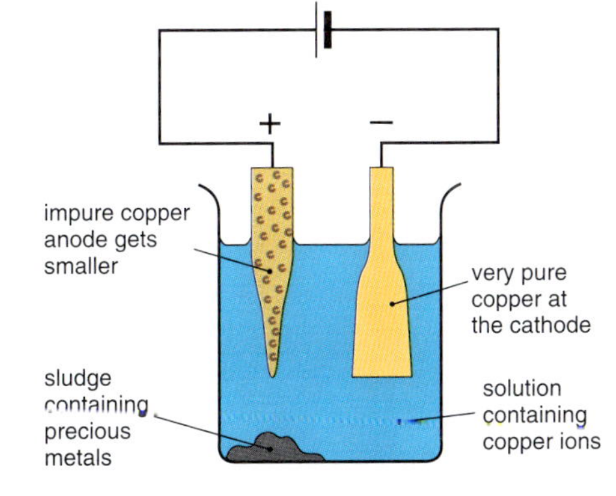

H

During electrolysis, reactions at the negative electrode (cathode) are called reduction:

e.g. $Al^{3+} + 3e^- \longrightarrow Al$
$Cu^{2+} + 2e^- \longrightarrow Cu$

Reduction is the gain of electrons.

Whilst at the positive electrode (anode), oxidation takes place:

e.g. $2O^{2-} \longrightarrow O_2 + 4e^-$
$Cu \longrightarrow Cu^{2+} + 2e^-$

Oxidation is the loss of electrons.

In chemical reactions, if one substance is reduced another is always oxidised; so the reactions are called **redox** reactions.

More in ***Chemistry for You***, pages 79–117.

Examination Questions – Useful products from metal ores

Year 10 questions

1 This question is about chemical processes.

Match words from the list with each of the examples **1**–**4** in the table.

electrolysis

neutralisation

oxidation

thermal decomposition

Process	Example of the process
1	Aluminium oxide splits into aluminium and oxygen when an electric current is passed through it
2	Calcium carbonate changes to calcium oxide and gives off carbon dioxide when it is heated
3	Carbon monoxide reacts with oxygen to form carbon dioxide
4	Sodium hydroxide reacts with hydrochloric acid to form sodium chloride and water

2 This question is about the reactivity series.

Carbon will displace metals **K** and **L** from their oxides.

Hydrogen will displace metal **K** from its oxide but cannot displace metal **L** from its oxide.

Carbon will not displace metals **M** and **N** from their oxides.

Metal **M** will displace metal **N** from its oxide.

Match metals from the list with each of the numbers **1**–**4** in the reactivity series.

metal K = number ....

metal L = number ....

metal M = number ....

metal N = number ....

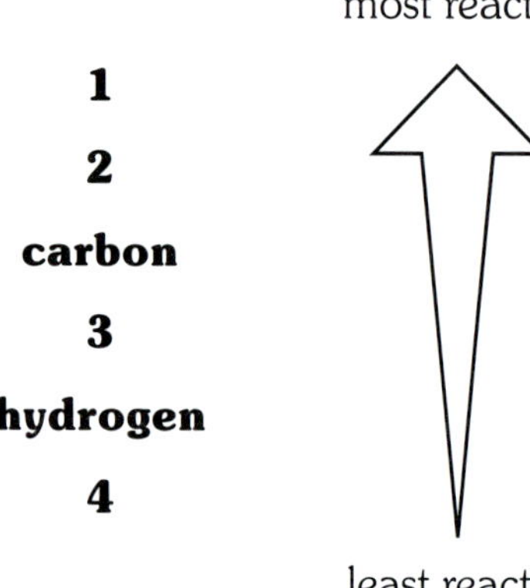

Year 11 questions

(You need to have covered Topics 13, 15 and 18 to answer these questions.)

1 Iron is the most commonly used metal. Iron is extracted in a blast furnace from iron oxide using carbon monoxide.

$$Fe_2O_3 + 3CO \longrightarrow 2Fe + 3CO_2$$

a) A sample of the ore haematite contains 70% iron oxide. Marks
Calculate the amount of iron oxide in 2000 tonnes of haematite.

....

....

Amount of iron oxide = ... tonnes

(1 mark)

b) Calculate the amount of iron that can be extracted from 2000 tonnes of haematite.

(Relative atomic masses: O = 16; Fe = 56)

....

....

....

....

....

Amount of iron = ... tonnes

(3 mark) 4

2 Aluminium oxide (Al_2O_3) is an ionic compound. It has a very high melting point.

a) Explain why ionic compounds have high melting points.

....

....

....

(1 mark)

b) The diagram shows the atoms that form aluminium oxide.

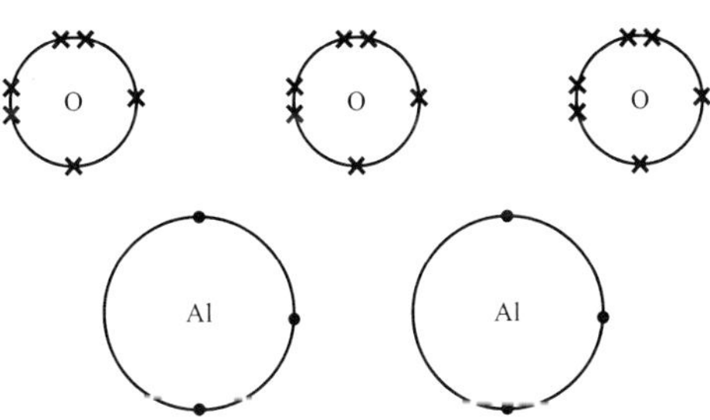

On the diagram, show the movements of electrons that occur to form aluminium oxide from these atoms. *(3 marks)*

c) Aluminium is manufactured by the electrolysis of molten aluminium oxide.
Balance the half equation for the reaction at the negative electrode.

$$Al^{3+} + e^{-} \longrightarrow Al$$ *(1 mark)* 5

3 Acids, alkalis and salts

ThinkAbout:

1 What is the name of the indicator we use to find the pH of a solution?

2 What is the colour of the indicator in question 1 in:
   a) a strongly acidic solution
   b) a strongly alkaline solution
   c) a neutral solution?

3 What is the pH of a neutral solution?

4 We can extract salt from rock salt. Put the steps below into the correct order:
   A Evaporate off the water.
   B Add water, stir.
   C Crush the rock salt.
   D Filter the mixture.

Neutralisation

We can **neutralise** an acid by reacting it with a base.
Alkalis are bases that can dissolve in water.
Acids form **hydrogen ions**, $H^+(aq)$, and alkalis form **hydroxide ions**, $OH^-(aq)$.
The general equation for a neutralisation reaction is:

acid + a base (or alkali) ⟶ a salt + water

For example,

hydrochloric acid	+	sodium hydroxide	⟶	sodium chloride	+	water
$HCl(aq)$	+	$NaOH(aq)$	⟶	$NaCl(aq)$	+	$H_2O(l)$

Ionic equations

H

We can summarise what happens when an acid and alkali neutralise each other with an ionic equation:

$$H^+(aq) + OH^-(aq) \longrightarrow H_2O(l)$$

An ionic equation only shows the ions that change in the reaction.

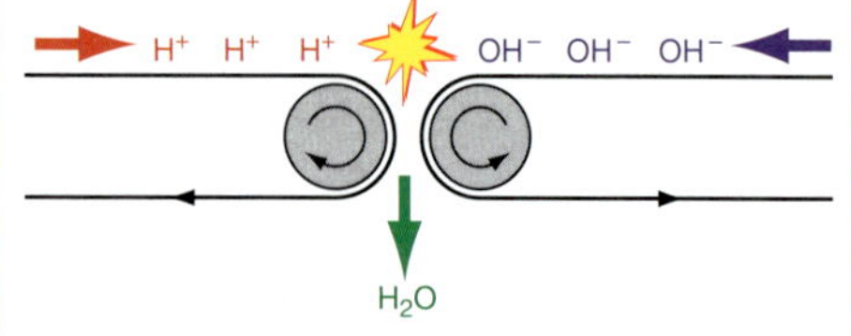

Salts

The salt made when we neutralise an acid depends on:

- the acid used, and
- the metal in the base or alkali.

The salt gets the first part of its name from the metal.
The last part of its name comes from the acid.

Hydrochloric acid (HCl) makes salts called **chlorides**.
Nitric acid (HNO_3) makes salts called **nitrates**.
Sulphuric acid (H_2SO_4) makes salts called **sulphates**.

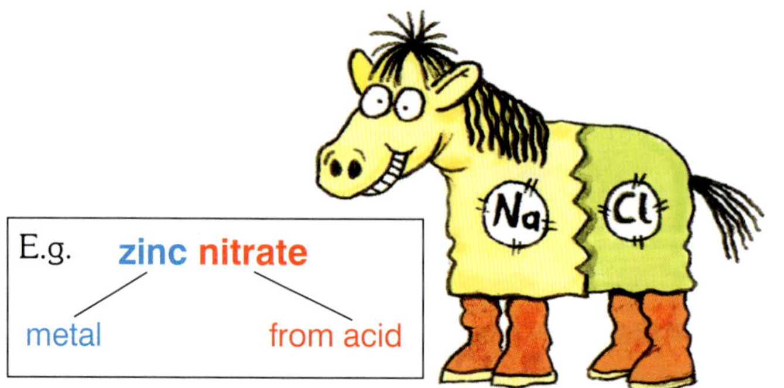

A salt is a metal plus the 'back-end' of an acid.

Answers: **1** universal indicator **2** a) red b) purple c) green **3** 7 **4** C, B, D, then A

Preparing salts

We can make crystals of metal salts from acids.

With an insoluble base, such as a transition metal oxide or hydroxide (such as copper oxide), we can filter off the excess base after the acid has been neutralised.

Then we evaporate off some of the water from the salt solution and leave it long enough for the crystals to form.

With an alkali we have to use an indicator to see when the acid has been neutralised.

D

Take care:

Most of the salts you meet will start their names with a metal. However, salts formed from the alkali, ammonia (NH_3) form **ammonium salts**. Examples are ammonium nitrate and ammonium sulphate.

Making copper sulphate in the lab

D

Step 1

- Pour $25\,cm^3$ of sulphuric acid into a small beaker.
- Add a spatula of copper oxide.

Step 2

- Stir with a glass rod.
- Add more copper oxide, one spatula at a time, until it no longer dissolves.
- Warm the mixture gently.

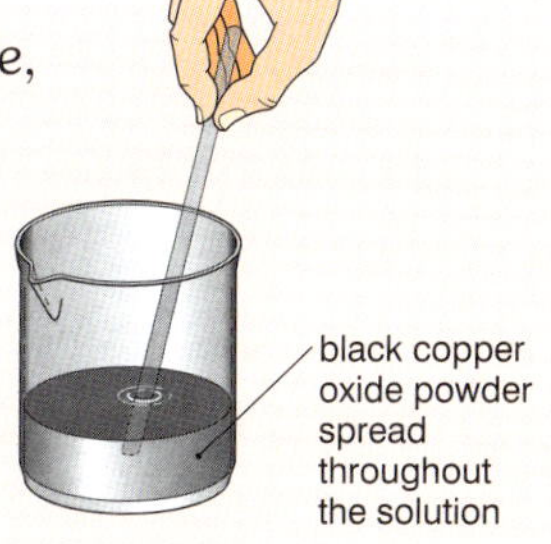

Step 3

- Filter off any un-reacted copper oxide.

Step 4

- Pour the solution from the flask into an evaporating dish.
- Then heat on a beaker of water, as shown here. Stop heating when you see some small crystals form around the edge of your solution.
- Leave your solution for a few days to form larger crystals.

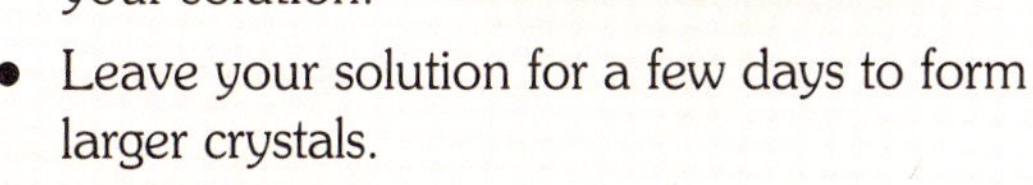

copper oxide + sulphuric acid ⟶ copper sulphate + water

More in ***Chemistry for You,*** pages 142–48.

Examination Questions – Acids, alkalis and salts

Year 10 questions

1 Which **two** of the following substances dissolve in water to form alkaline solutions?

aluminium chloride

ammonia

copper

iron hydroxide

sodium hydroxide

2 You can make a solution of a salt by reacting an acid with an alkali.

2.1 Which salt is produced in this reaction?

ammonia solution + nitric acid ⟶ ....**?**.............. + water

A ammonia

B ammonium chloride

C ammonium nitrate

D ammonium sulphate

2.2 When the ammonia solution is completely neutralised by the nitric acid solution, the reaction can be written …

A $H^-(aq) + OH^+(aq) \longrightarrow H_2O(l)$

B $H^+(aq) + OH^-(aq) \longrightarrow H_2O(l)$

C $H^+(aq) - OH^-(aq) \longrightarrow H_2O(l)$

D $H^-(aq) - OH^-(aq) \longrightarrow H_2O(l)$

2.3 A molecule of nitric acid (HNO_3) has one hydrogen atom which can be replaced by a metal to form a normal salt. When the acid molecule has two or more replaceable hydrogen atoms, normal or acid salts may be formed.

Which one of these acids will form acid salts?

A carbonic acid, H_2CO_3

B hydriodic acid, HI

C hydrobromic acid, HBr

D hydrochloric acid, HCl

2.4 Which of these substances will react with nitric acid to produce the salt, copper nitrate?

A copper bromide

B copper chloride

C copper oxide

D copper sulphate

Year 11 questions

1 Four solutions, **A, B, C** and **D** are tested with universal indicator.

The table shows the results of these tests.

Solution	pH
A	5–6
B	13–14
C	7
D	1

a) Which solution is: Marks

i alkaline? ....

ii most strongly acidic? ....

iii weakly acidic? ....

(3 marks)

b) Solution **B** is added to solution **D** until the indicator is green.

i What does this tell you about the mixture of **B** and **D**? Underline the correct answer.

It is ...

strongly acidic

weakly acidic

neutral

weakly alkaline

strongly alkaline *(1 mark)*

ii What do we call the type of reaction between solution **B** and solution **D**?

....

(1 mark)

iii What **two** new substances are produced when solutions **B** and **D** are mixed?

....

and

....

(2 marks) 7

Getting the Grades – Metals

Try this question, then compare your answer with the two examples opposite ▶

1 You may find tables 1 and 2 (see page 117) on the data sheet helpful in answering this question. This question is about the extraction of aluminium from its ore. The extraction process involves the electrolysis of aluminium oxide in a cell like the one shown below:

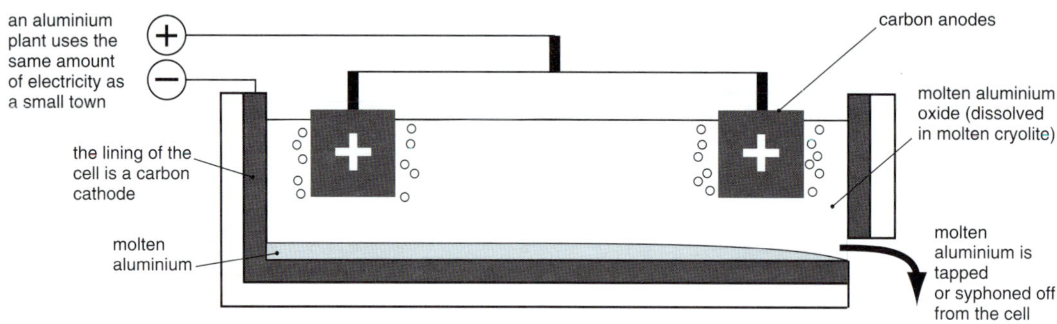

a) Iron can be extracted from iron oxide by heating with carbon in the form of coke. Why is it not possible to use carbon to extract aluminium from its oxide?

....

.... (2 marks)

b) What do you understand by the term 'electrolysis'?

....

.... (2 marks)

c) Use the list below to complete the following passage. Each word should be used once:

reduced, cathode, electrode, ions, anode

In the electrolysis of aluminium oxide the positively charged aluminium .... *are attracted to the* .... *and migrate towards it. At this* .... *each of these ions receives electrons and are thus* .... *to aluminium atoms. The carbon, of which the* .... *is made, gets burned away as the oxygen produced combines with it.* (2 marks)

d) Explain in terms of the behaviour of particles, why the aluminium oxide needs to be melted.

....

.... (2 marks)

e) Write an equation to represent the chemical changes which take place at the cathode.

.... (2 marks)

f) Suggest why aluminium is an expensive metal to produce.

....

.... (2 marks)

g) Explain why, despite the expense, aluminium is a very useful metal.

....

.... (2 marks)

[*Total 14 marks*]

GRADE 'A' ANSWER

1 a) Aluminium is more reactive than carbon ✓

b) Electrolysis involves the breakdown ✓ of a chemical substance by an electric current ✓

Note that electrolysis leads to chemical changes in the substance being electrolysed

c) ions cathode ✓ electrode
reduced ✓ anode ✓

d) Heating melts the electrolyte enabling the ions to become mobile ✓, so they can migrate and therefore conduct an electric current ✓

e) $Al^{3+} + e^- \rightarrow Al$ ✓ ✗

The candidate has shown reduction but given the wrong number of electrons ($Al^{3+} + 3e^- \longrightarrow Al$)

f) A lot of electricity ✓ and heating is required in order to extract it from its ore ✓

g) Aluminium has a tough layer of corrosion resistant oxide on its surface ✓

The candidate has not referred to the fact that Aluminium can be made into strong alloys

12 marks = Grade A answer

Improve your Grades A up to A*

When writing equations in examination questions be sure to double check them before submitting your paper. Use your text book to draw up and learn a list of the uses of aluminium. In each case try to decide which property of the metal makes it suitable for the particular use.

GRADE 'C' ANSWER

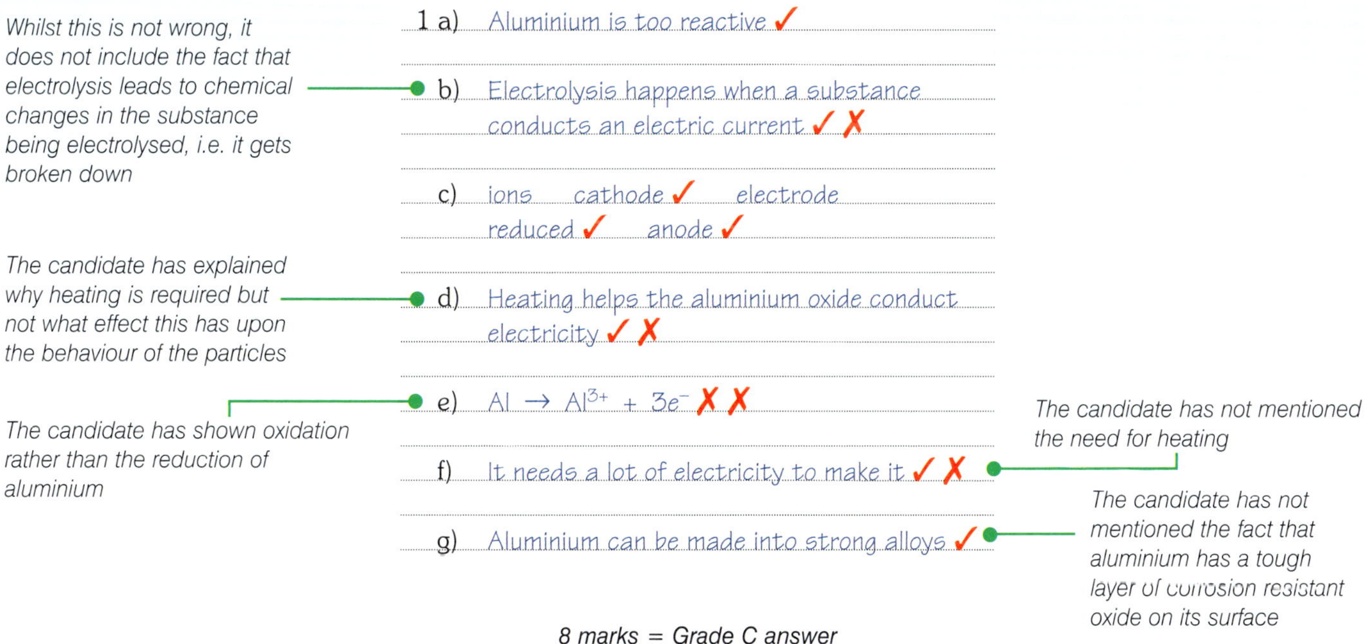

1 a) Aluminium is too reactive ✓

b) Electrolysis happens when a substance conducts an electric current ✓ ✗

Whilst this is not wrong, it does not include the fact that electrolysis leads to chemical changes in the substance being electrolysed, i.e. it gets broken down

c) ions cathode ✓ electrode
reduced ✓ anode ✓

d) Heating helps the aluminium oxide conduct electricity ✓ ✗

The candidate has explained why heating is required but not what effect this has upon the behaviour of the particles

e) $Al \rightarrow Al^{3+} + 3e^-$ ✗ ✗

The candidate has shown oxidation rather than the reduction of aluminium

f) It needs a lot of electricity to make it ✓ ✗

The candidate has not mentioned the need for heating

g) Aluminium can be made into strong alloys ✓

The candidate has not mentioned the fact that aluminium has a tough layer of corrosion resistant oxide on its surface

8 marks = Grade C answer

Improve your Grades C up to B

Remember that your data sheet has details of ionic charges and reactivities. These ideas are often helpful in questions to do with the extraction of metals from their ores.

Try to learn the details of the industrial electrolysis of aluminium oxide. A sketch diagram with careful labels will help. Use equations to explain the processes which take place at the electrodes. (See page 83.)

4 USEFUL PRODUCTS FROM

ThinkAbout:

1 Name three rocks that are made mainly from calcium carbonate.

2 What do we call the reaction between an acid and an alkali?

3 a) Which gas is given off when calcium carbonate reacts with acid?

b) How would you test for this gas?

Limestone

Limestone is made up mainly of **calcium carbonate** ($CaCO_3$). It is used as a building material itself, but is also used to make **cement**.
Powdered limestone is heated in a rotating kiln with clay (or shale) to make the cement.

Cement is the basis of **concrete** – the most widely used building material. This is made by mixing cement, sand and crushed rock, together with water. The mixture sets in a slow chemical reaction to form a very hard, rock-like substance.

The lime kiln

When we heat limestone in a lime kiln it makes quicklime (calcium oxide, CaO):

$$CaCO_3(s) \longrightarrow CaO(s) + CO_2(g)$$

The reaction is called **thermal decomposition**.

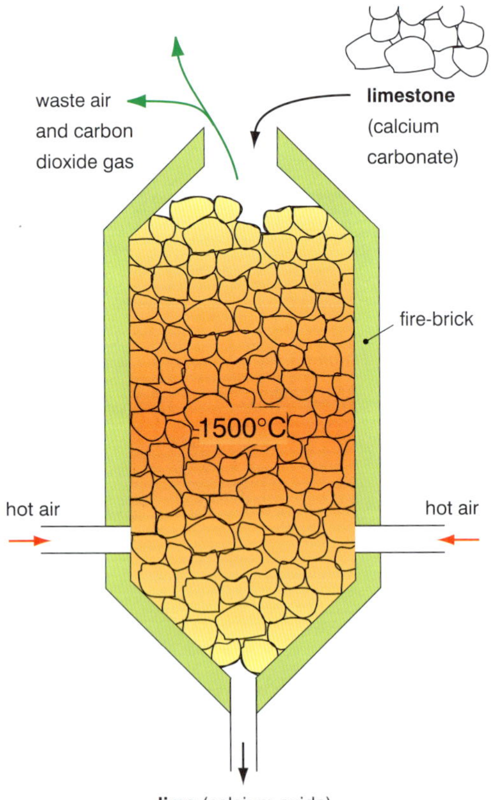

By adding water to quicklime, we get slaked lime (calcium hydroxide, $Ca(OH)_2$) which is a cheap alkali. This, or powdered limestone, can be used to raise the pH of acidic soil.

Powdered limestone is also used to neutralise lakes affected by acid rain.

Answers: 1 limestone, chalk and marble 2 neutralisation 3 a) carbon dioxide b) limewater turns milky

Glass

We make glass by heating sand, limestone and soda (sodium carbonate).

D

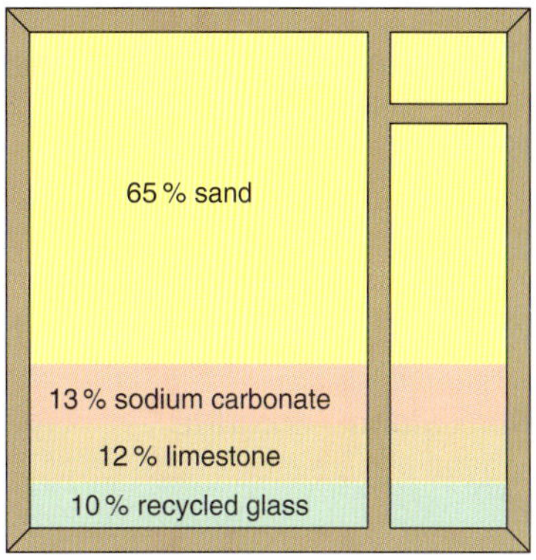

65 % sand
13 % sodium carbonate
12 % limestone
10 % recycled glass

Uses of limestone

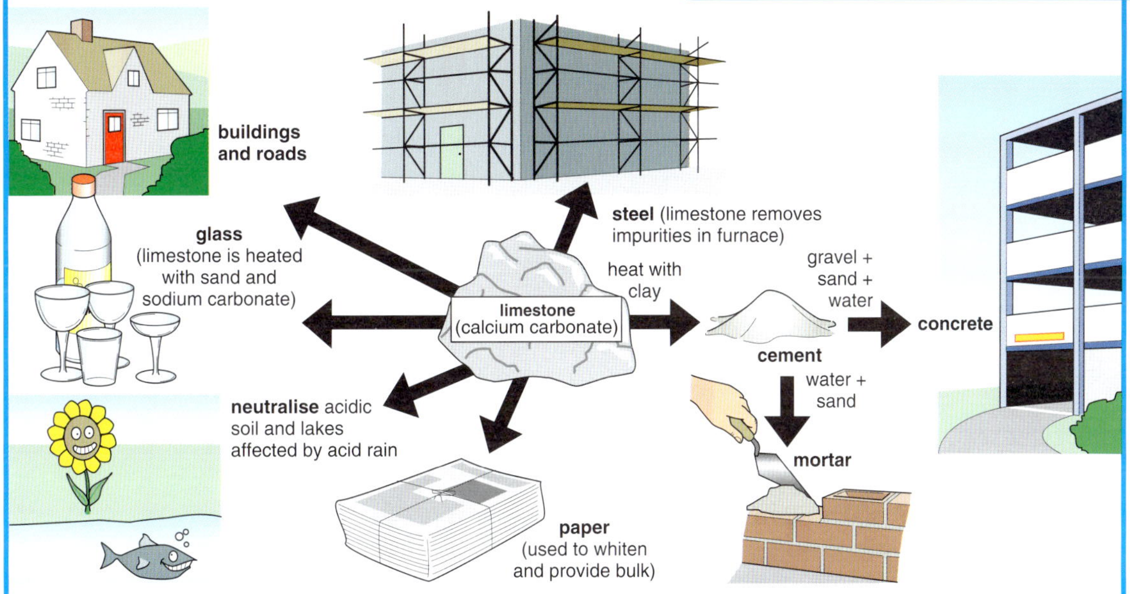

buildings and roads
glass (limestone is heated with sand and sodium carbonate)
steel (limestone removes impurities in furnace)
heat with clay
limestone (calcium carbonate)
cement
gravel + sand + water
concrete
water + sand
mortar
neutralise acidic soil and lakes affected by acid rain
paper (used to whiten and provide bulk)

Reactions of limestone

calcium carbonate
limestone
step 1
heat
carbon dioxide given off
calcium oxide
lime or quicklime
step 2
add a little water
calcium hydroxide
slaked lime
step 3
add more water and filter
calcium hydroxide solution
limewater
step 4
add carbon dioxide (this is the test for CO_2)

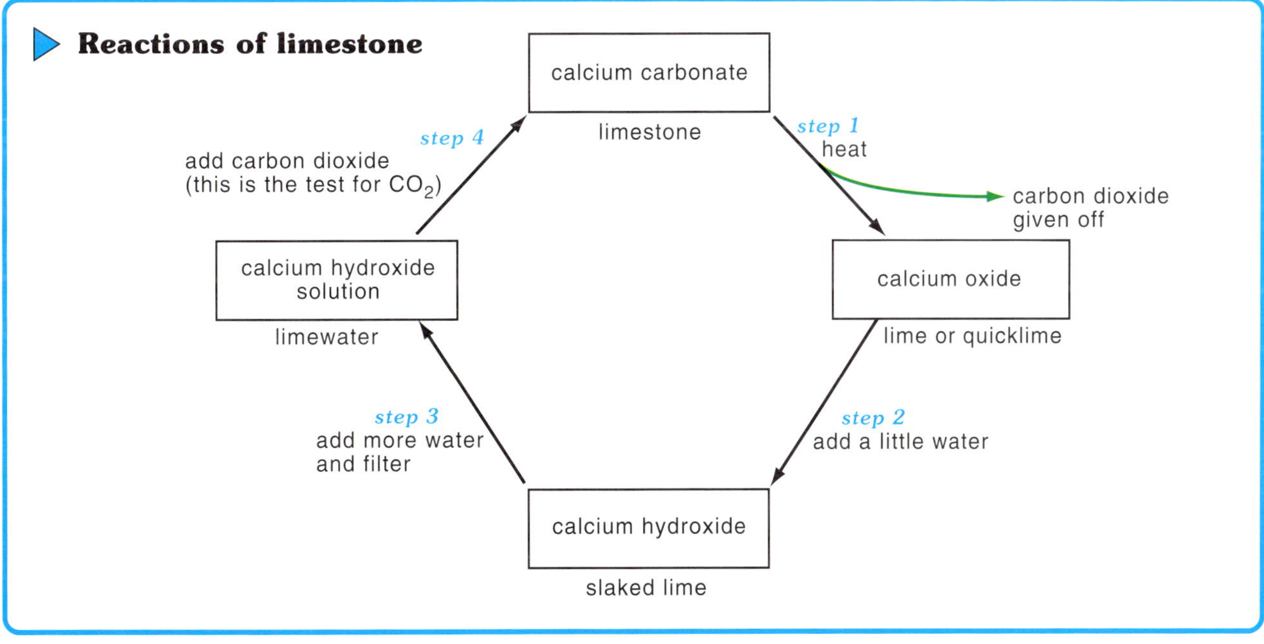

More in ***Chemistry for You***, pages 127–134.

Examination Questions – Useful products from rocks

Year 10 questions

1 1.1 The word equation shows the breakdown of limestone when it is heated in a lime kiln.

calcium carbonate ⟶ .... **?**............... + carbon dioxide

Which substance completes the word equation?

A calcium chloride

B calcium hydrogencarbonate

C calcium hydroxide

D calcium oxide

1.2 Powdered limestone can be mixed with powdered clay and heated in a rotary kiln.

The main useful product is …

A cement.

B concrete.

C glass.

D quicklime.

1.3 The chemical name for slaked lime is …

A calcium chloride.

B calcium hydroxide.

C calcium oxide.

D calcium sulphate.

1.4 One use of slaked lime is to …

A make concrete.

B make quicklime.

C make soil less acidic.

D neutralise alkaline lake water.

2 The diagram shows stages in making cement and concrete.

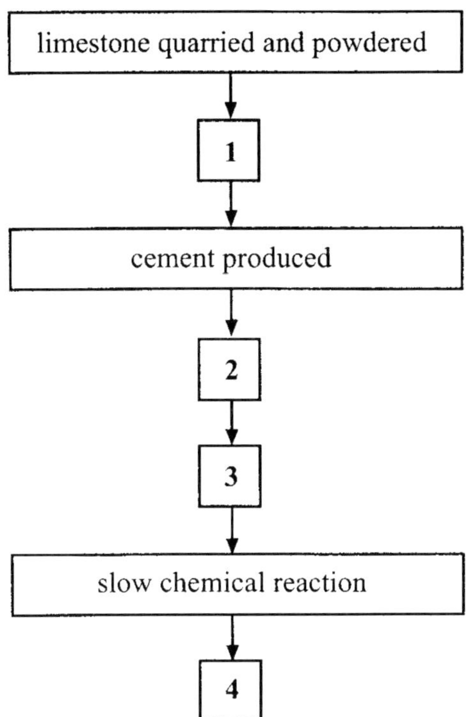

Match words from the list with each of the spaces **1–4**, to describe what happens in this process.

Cement mixed with sand and crushed rock

Concrete produced

Limestone heated in a kiln with clay

Water added to mixture

3 What is the main compound found in all limestones?

A Calcium carbonate

B Calcium oxide

C Calcium sulphate

D Calcium hydroxide

4 Which one of the following describes the type of reaction that takes place in a lime kiln?

A Oxidation

B Electrolysis

C Thermal decomposition

D Neutralisation

5

USEFUL PRODUCTS FROM OIL

ThinkAbout:

1 Finish this sentence:
Crude oil is a …
A mixture of elements
B mixture of compounds
C pure compound
D pure element.

2 What is a hydrocarbon?

3 Crude oil is a fossil fuel. Name two others.

4 Finish this sentence:
We find crude oil beneath layers of s… rock.

5 Why didn't the animals and plants that formed fossil fuels just rot away when they died?

Crude oil

Most of the compounds in crude oil are called **hydrocarbons**. They contain only hydrogen and carbon atoms.

> Crude oil contains a **mixture of hydrocarbons**.

(A mixture consists of two or more elements or compounds that are *not* chemically combined. The substances in the mixture still have their original properties. This allows them to be separated.)

The hydrocarbons in crude oil all have different boiling points. They can be separated into compounds with similar boiling points by **fractional distillation**.

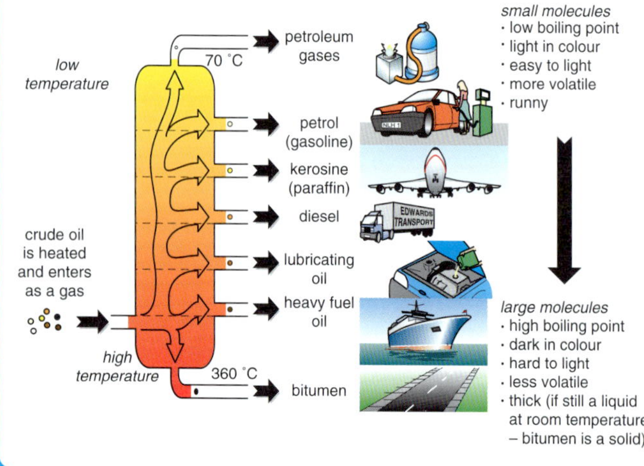

Alkanes

H

> Many of the hydrocarbons in crude oil are called **alkanes**.

Their molecules contain only single bonds. They are known as **saturated** hydrocarbons.

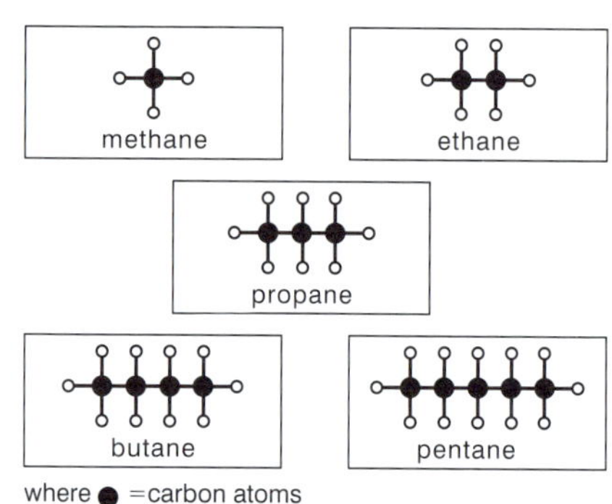

Cracking

Most of the fractions from crude oil are used as fuels.

Fuels such as petrol are in great demand.

So some large hydrocarbon molecules in the heavier fractions are **'cracked'** into smaller, more useful molecules to use as fuels.

For example:

$$\text{decane} \longrightarrow \text{octane} + \text{ethene}$$
$$C_{10}H_{22} \longrightarrow C_8H_{18} + C_2H_4$$

The large molecules are heated and passed over a catalyst to break them down.

Cracking is an example of a **thermal decomposition** reaction.

Answers:

1 B, mixture of compounds **2** a compound containing only hydrogen and carbon atoms
3 natural gas and coal **4** sedimentary **5** There was no air/oxygen present where they came to rest.

Polymers

During cracking, we also get small reactive molecules, such as ethene, formed.
These can react with each other when heated under pressure.

In the presence of a catalyst, these molecules join together to make large molecules used to make plastics.

> The small molecules are called **monomers**.
> The large molecule they form is called a **polymer**.
> The reaction is called **addition polymerisation.**

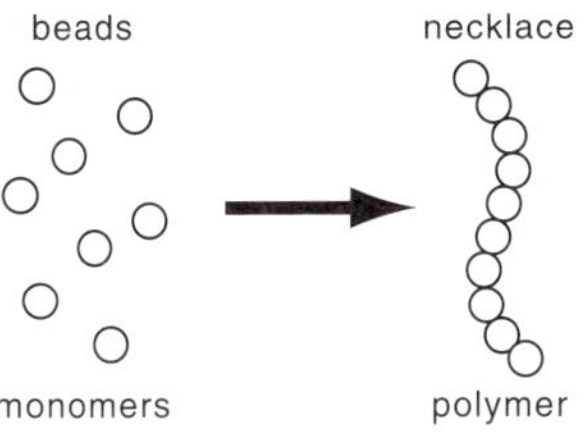

Some uses of plastics

poly(ethene)

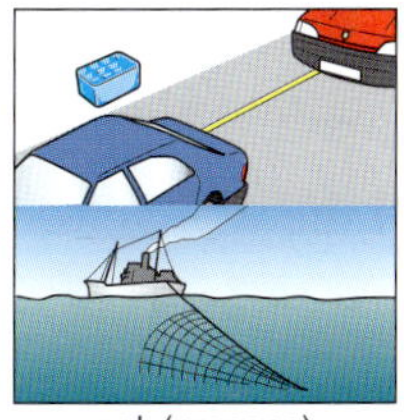
poly(propene)

The trouble with plastics and fuels

There is a problem disposing of plastics because when thrown away many are not broken down by micro-organisms in the soil.
We are also concerned about air pollution caused by burning fuels:

- When a hydrocarbon burns we get carbon dioxide (causing the **greenhouse effect**) and water vapour.
- Impurities of sulphur in the fuels also produce sulphur dioxide gas (causing **acid rain**).

The structure of ethene is:

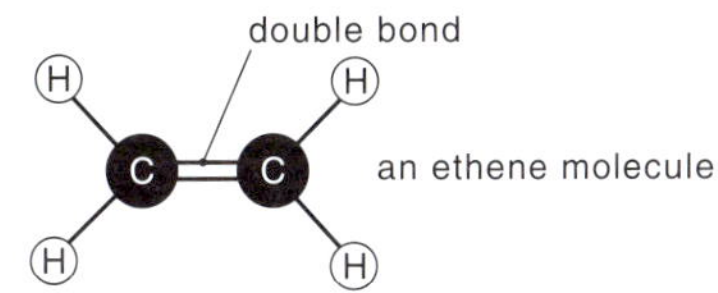

Ethene is the smallest member of a group of hydrocarbons called **alkenes**. They all contain at least one carbon–carbon double bond and are known as **unsaturated** hydrocarbons.

The double bond 'opens up' in its reactions and new atoms bond to each carbon atom in **addition reactions**.

We can think of the polymerisation reaction as shown opposite:

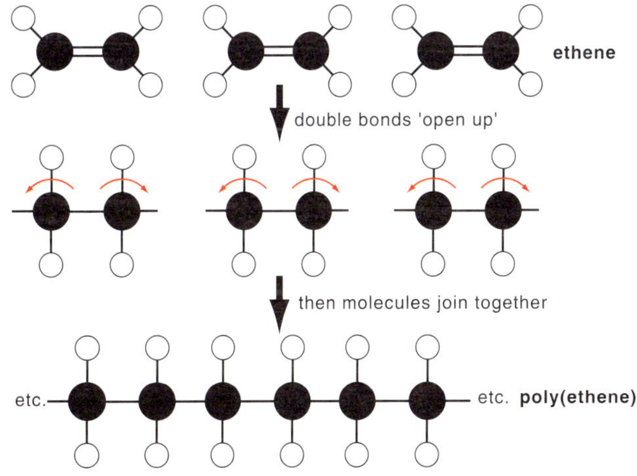

This can be represented in an equation:

$$n\,C_2H_4 \longrightarrow \left(C_2H_4 \right)_n$$

poly(ethene),
often called polythene

You can test for an unsaturated compound by adding bromine water (yellow), which turns colourless. For example, with ethene:

$$C_2H_4 + Br_2 \longrightarrow C_2H_4Br_2$$

Take care:
Fractional distillation involves physical changes, whereas cracking involves chemical changes.

More in ***Chemistry for You***, pages 159–177.

Examination Questions – Useful products from oil

Year 10 questions

1 The diagram shows stages in the cracking of hydrocarbons.

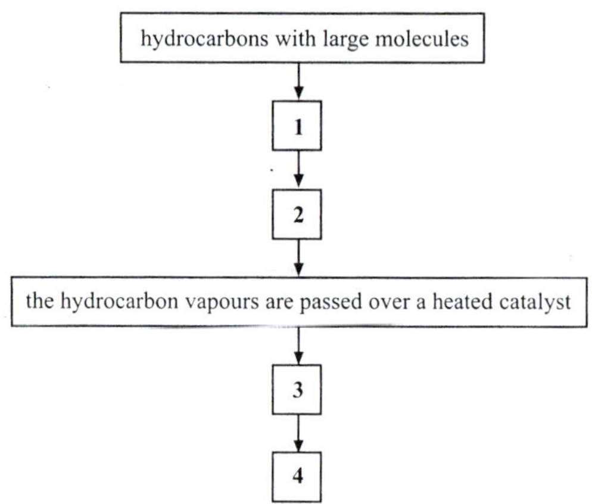

Match the words from the list with each of the spaces **1–4**, to describe what happens in this process.

Hydrocarbons with small molecules

The hydrocarbons are heated

The hydrocarbons are in a vapour state

Thermal decomposition of hydrocarbons

2 In a fractionating column, crude oil is separated into a number of fractions, some of which are shown in the diagram.

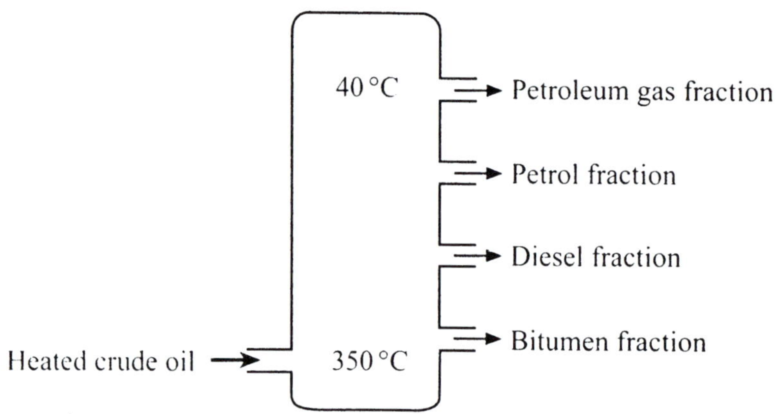

2.1 Crude oil is …

A a compound of carbon and hydrogen only.

B a mixture of cements.

C a mixture of hydrocarbons.

D an element.

2.2 The hydrocarbon molecules in each fraction contain …

A a similar number of carbon atoms.

B a similar number of oxygen atoms.

C carbon, hydrogen and oxygen atoms.

D exactly the same number of carbon atoms.

2.3 Hydrocarbon molecules vary in size.
The fraction containing hydrocarbons with the smallest molecules is …….

A the bitumen fraction.

B the diesel fraction.

C the petrol fraction.

D the petroleum gas fraction.

2.4 When compared with other hydrocarbons, those with the smallest molecules ….

A will be easier to ignite.

B will be less volatile.

C will be more viscous.

D will have higher boiling points.

Year 11 questions

1 The many hydrocarbons in crude oil are separated into fractions.

a) Some of the larger hydrocarbon molecules can be broken down to produce smaller, more useful hydrocarbon molecules.

Marks

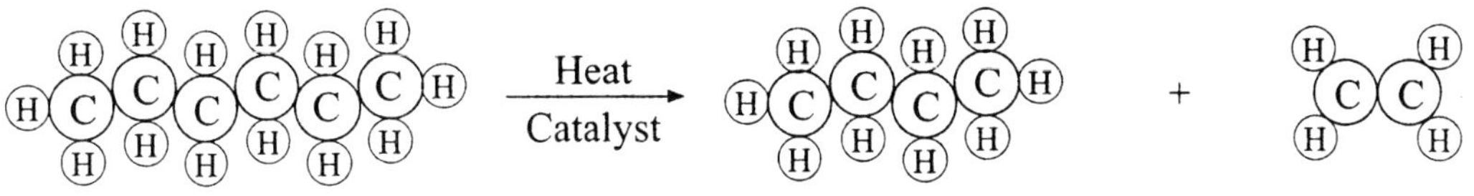

Hexane —Heat / Catalyst→ Butane + Ethene

Hexane and butane are alkanes. Describe the structure of alkanes.

(3 marks)

b) Ethene is used to make poly(ethene).

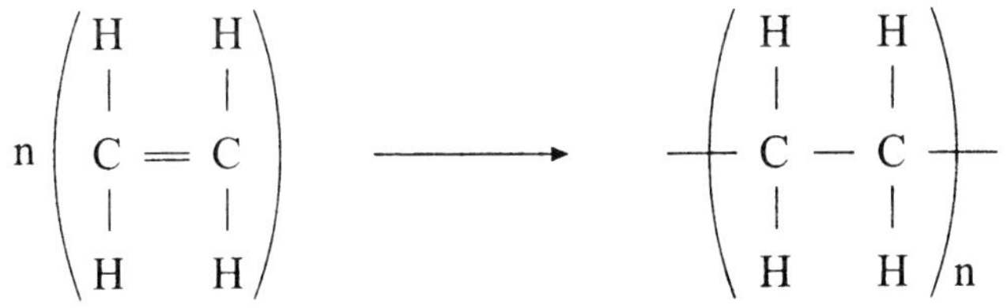

Ethene → Poly(ethene)

This process is called polymerisation. Explain what is meant by polymerisation.

(2 marks) 5

6 Changes to the Atmosphere

ThinkAbout:

1 Name the main noble gas found in the air.

2 Why are people worried about increasing levels of carbon dioxide in the atmosphere?

3 What is the formula of:
a) oxygen gas b) nitrogen gas
c) argon gas?

D

The atmosphere

The air is made up of about:
- 80% nitrogen gas
- 20% oxygen gas
- small amounts of other gases, including carbon dioxide, water vapour and noble gases.

History of the atmosphere

In the Earth's first billion years, its early atmosphere came from volcanoes.
It was probably mainly **carbon dioxide** (like Mars and Venus now).
There was no oxygen. This only arrived once the first plants had evolved.
During photosynthesis, the plants took in carbon dioxide and gave out oxygen.

Most carbon became 'trapped' in fossil fuels and carbonate rocks.
The oceans were formed when water vapour from the volcanoes fell as rain as the Earth cooled down.

The small amount of ammonia and methane in the early atmosphere was removed when they reacted with oxygen gas.

The history of our atmosphere

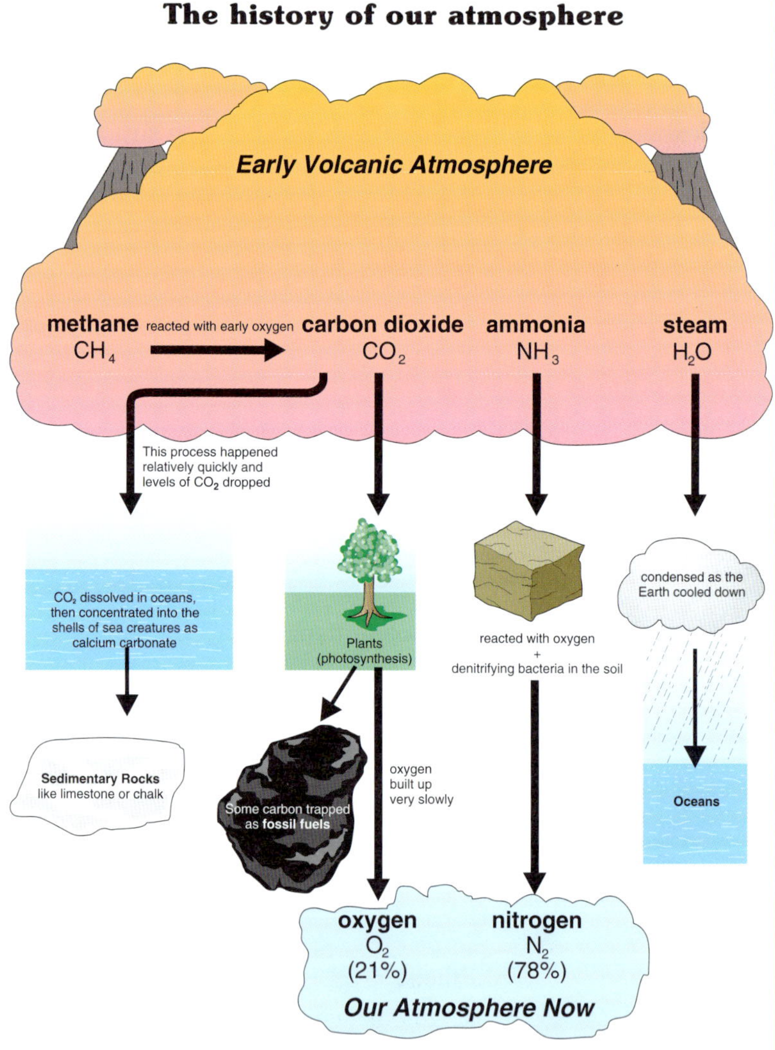

Most nitrogen in the atmosphere came from the action of **denitrifying bacteria** in the soil.
Some of the oxygen gas (O_2) in the air was converted to ozone gas (O_3). This formed the **ozone layer** in the upper atmosphere. This was an important stage in life developing on land.

D

The **ozone layer** protects the surface of the Earth from harmful ultraviolet radiation arriving from the Sun.

Answers: **1** argon **2** global warming/greenhouse effect **3** a) O_2 b) N_2 c) Ar

▶ The carbon cycle

The natural balance of carbon dioxide in the atmosphere is maintained in the carbon cycle:

D **H**

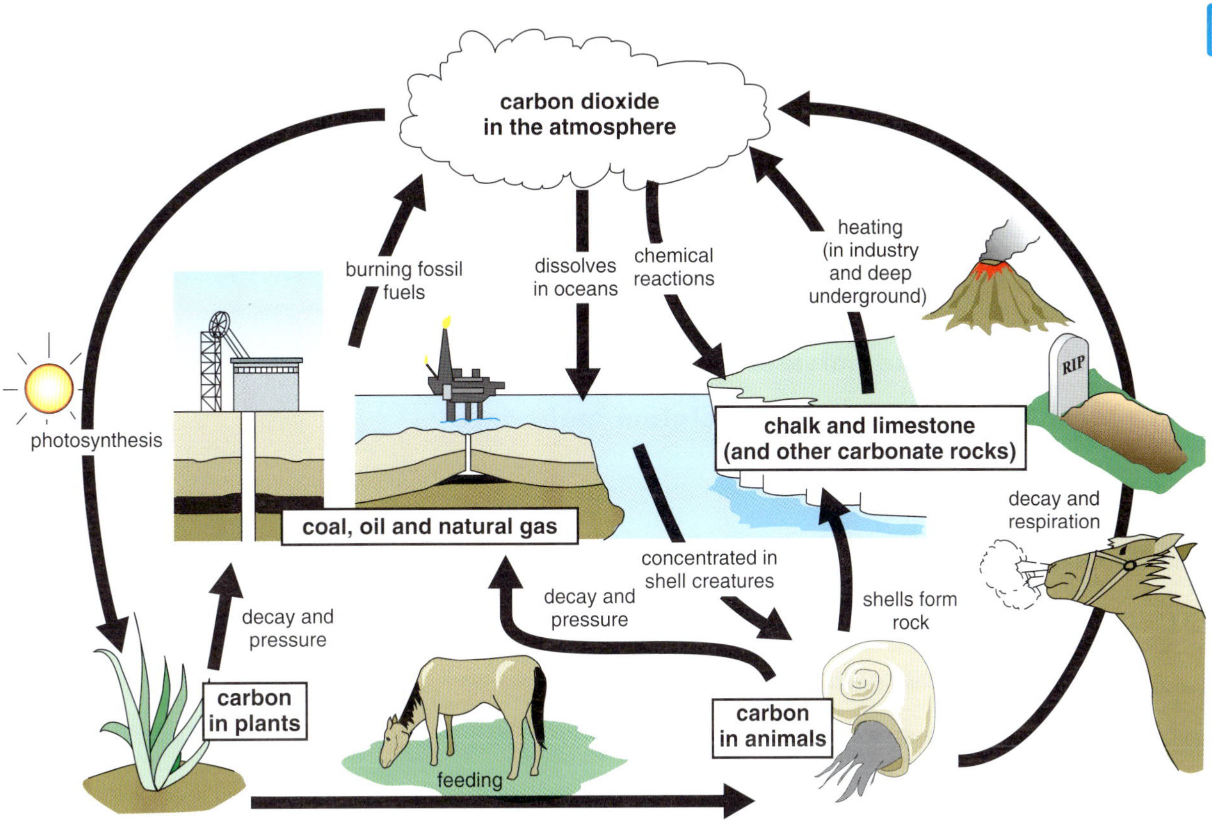

carbon dioxide in the atmosphere
burning fossil fuels
dissolves in oceans
chemical reactions
heating (in industry and deep underground)
photosynthesis
coal, oil and natural gas
chalk and limestone (and other carbonate rocks)
decay and respiration
concentrated in shell creatures
decay and pressure
shells form rock
decay and pressure
carbon in plants
carbon in animals
feeding

The carbon cycle

D **H**

- The oceans act as a huge reservoir for carbon dioxide.
- The CO_2 gas reacts in the seawater to produce insoluble carbonates (which precipitate out as solids, such as calcium carbonate) and soluble hydrogencarbonates (such as those of calcium and magnesium).
- However, our burning of fossil fuels releases vast amounts of carbon dioxide into the atmosphere.
- As industrialisation increases, the oceans can no longer cope with the volumes of carbon dioxide (a 'greenhouse gas') produced.
- Most people are getting more and more concerned about the threat of global warming.

Take care:
The timescales involved in the history of the atmosphere are vast – the current proportions of gases have been roughly constant for the last 200 million years!

More in ***Chemistry for You***, pages 314–21.

Examination Questions – Changes to the atmosphere

Year 10 questions

1 This question is about carbon dioxide gas.

Which **two** statements about the gas are correct?

it is produced during the cracking of large hydrocarbon molecules

it is produced when quicklime reacts with water

it is released during thermal decomposition of carbonate rocks

it is released in the polymerisation of alkenes

it reacts in seawater to form calcium carbonate

2 The composition of the Earth's atmosphere has changed since it was first formed.

2.1 The Earth's early atmosphere was similar to the atmosphere of Venus today.

The main gas forming this atmosphere was …

A carbon dioxide.

B nitrogen.

C oxygen.

D ozone.

2.2 Most of the gas which formed this early atmosphere came from …

A the activity of plants.

B the condensation of water vapour.

C the eruption of volcanoes.

D the formation of fossil fuels.

2.3 The other gases making up this early atmosphere were …

A ammonia and carbon monoxide.

B ammonia and chlorine.

C ammonia, methane and water vapour.

D argon, carbon monoxide and chlorine.

2.4 The present day atmosphere is made up mainly of …

A carbon dioxide and nitrogen.

B carbon dioxide and oxygen.

C hydrogen and oxygen.

D nitrogen and oxygen.

3 This question is about gases.

Match words from the list with each of the numbers **1–4** in the table.

carbon dioxide

oxygen

sulphur dioxide

water vapour

Gas	What we can say about the gas
1	It is an oxide of hydrogen
2	It is formed when sulphur burns in air
3	It reacts with carbon to form carbon dioxide
4	It is produced in the thermal decomposition of copper carbonate

Year 11 questions

1 Look at the graph below: Marks

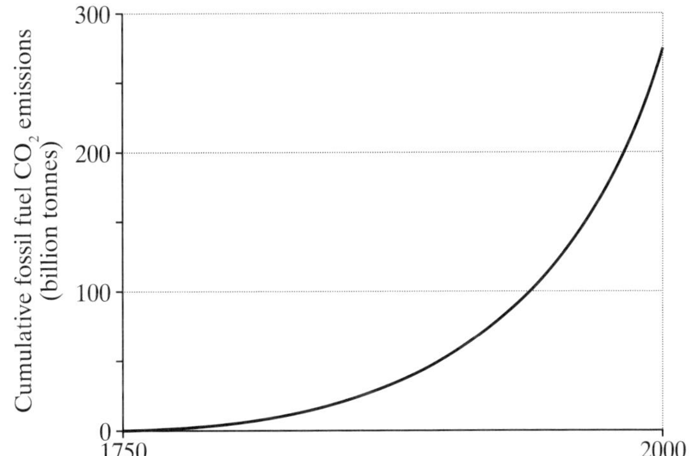

a) i Describe the trend shown on the graph.

....

....

(1 mark)

ii Explain this trend.

....

....

(1 mark)

b) Why are people increasingly concerned about the data shown on the graph?

....

....

(2 marks) 4

7 The rock record

▶ **ThinkAbout:**

1 Complete these examples of sedimentary rock:
c _ _ _ _   s _ _ _ _ _ _ _ _
m _ _ _ _ _ _ _   l _ _ _ _ _ _ _ _
c _ _ _ _ _ _ _ _ _ _ _ _

2 Complete these examples of metamorphic rock:
m _ _ _ _ _   s _ _ _ _

3 Complete these examples of igneous rock:
g _ _ _ _ _ _   b _ _ _ _ _

▶ Structure of the Earth

The Earth is made up from:

- a thin outer crust
- a mantle (under the crust stretching almost half-way to the centre of the Earth)
- a core (the outer core is liquid; the inner core is solid; both parts are made from iron and nickel).

The Earth's crust and uppermost part of its mantle (called the **lithosphere**) is split up into tectonic plates. These move very slowly on convection currents set up in the mantle. The heat comes from radioactive rocks.

We can work out the plate boundaries by looking at where we get earthquakes and volcanoes. (See Question 1 on page 37).

D

▶ Sedimentary rocks

D

Sedimentary rocks are formed when bits of rock, shell or plants settle in layers.

The rock contains evidence of how the sediment was originally deposited.

For example:

- Ripple marks show the direction of currents or waves.
- Sharp boundaries between neighbouring sedimentary layers indicate distinct periods when different sediments were laid down.
- Younger sedimentary rock usually lies on top of older rock.

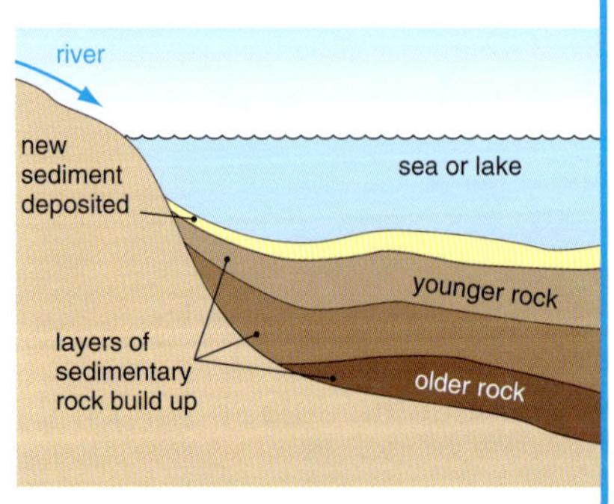

▶ Distorted layers

D

The layers of sedimentary rock are often found tilted, folded or fractured (faulted) by stress forces set up within the Earth's crust. Occasionally the layers can even be turned upside down. In this case the younger rock will lie beneath the older layers.

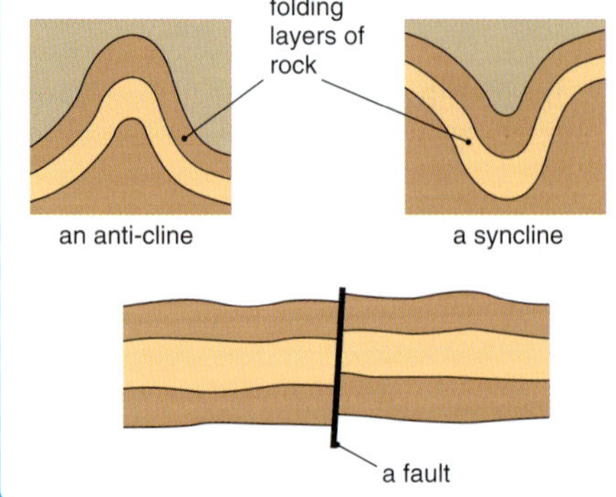

Answers: **1** chalk, sandstone, mudstone, limestone, conglomerate **2** marble, slate **3** granite, basalt

Metamorphic rocks

D

Metamorphic rocks are formed when rocks are put under great pressure and/or are heated to high temperatures (without melting).

Where the Earth's plates collide, mountains are built (replacing those worn away over millions of years by weathering and erosion).

Metamorphic rocks are found in these mountain ranges. This is due to the great pressure and high temperatures produced as mountains form.

Take care:

- Metamorphic rock formed under pressure will often have bands of minerals running through the rock. However those formed by heating, such as some marble from limestone, will not have bands.
- The crystals in metamorphic rocks are difficult to see because they are usually very small.

Plates moving towards each other

D H

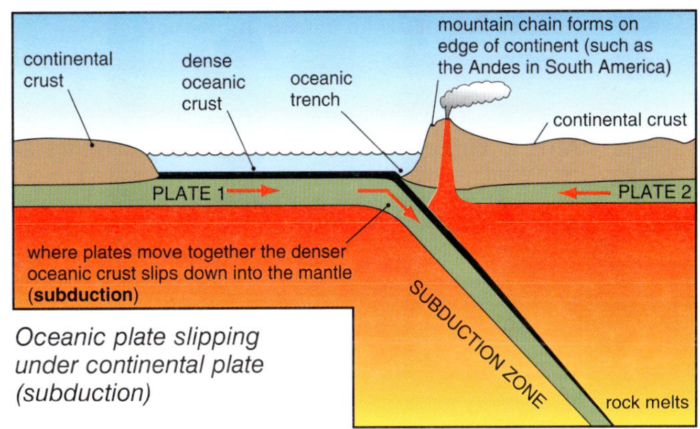

Oceanic plate slipping under continental plate (subduction)

Tectonic plates

D

The Earth's plates are moving at about the same rate as your fingernails grow!

Where plates slip past each other, we get earthquakes.

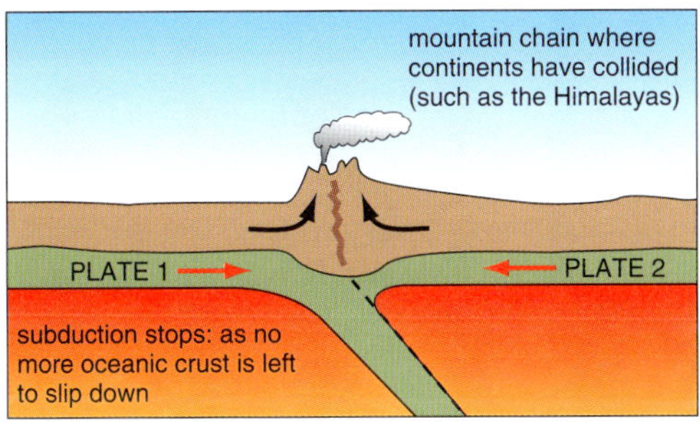

Continental plates colliding

Plates moving away from each other

D H

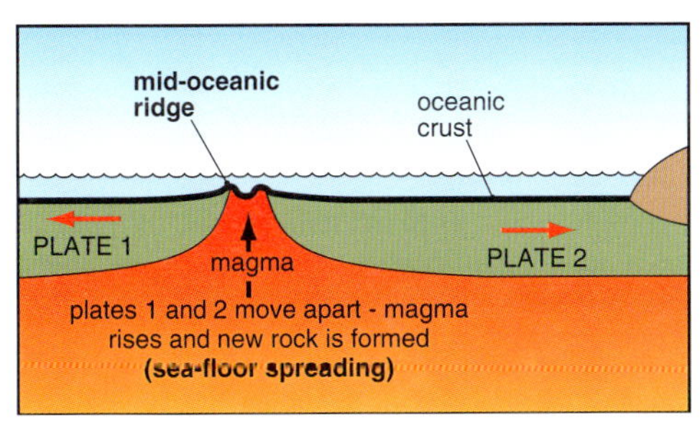

D H

The iron in the rocks on either side of a mid-oceanic ridge provide evidence for 'sea-floor spreading'.

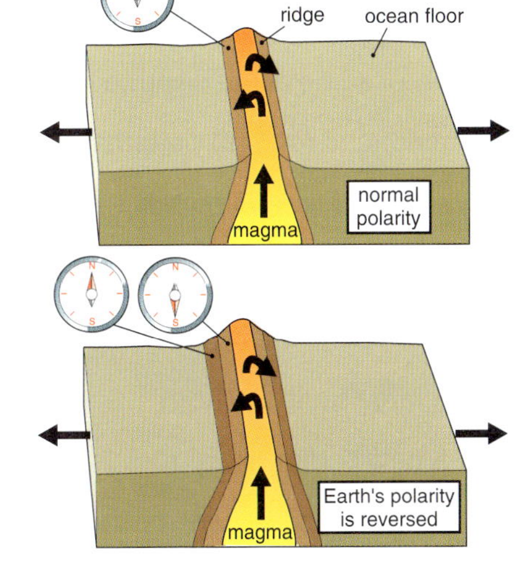

More in ***Chemistry for You***, pages 323–46.

Examination Questions – The rock record

Year 10 questions

1 This question is about rocks in the Earth's crust.

Match rock types from the list with each of the numbers **1–4** in the table.

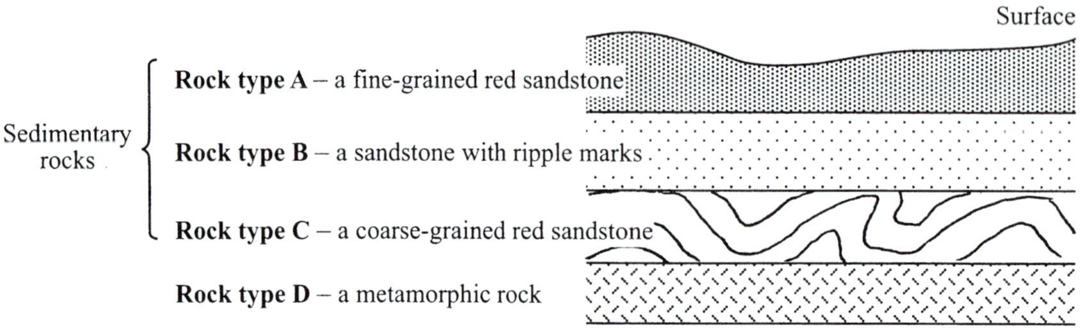

Rock type	What we can say about the rock
1	It has been folded
2	It is probably the youngest rock
3	It was formed under high temperature and pressure
4	It was deposited under water.

2 The diagram shows an oceanic plate and a continental plate moving towards each other.

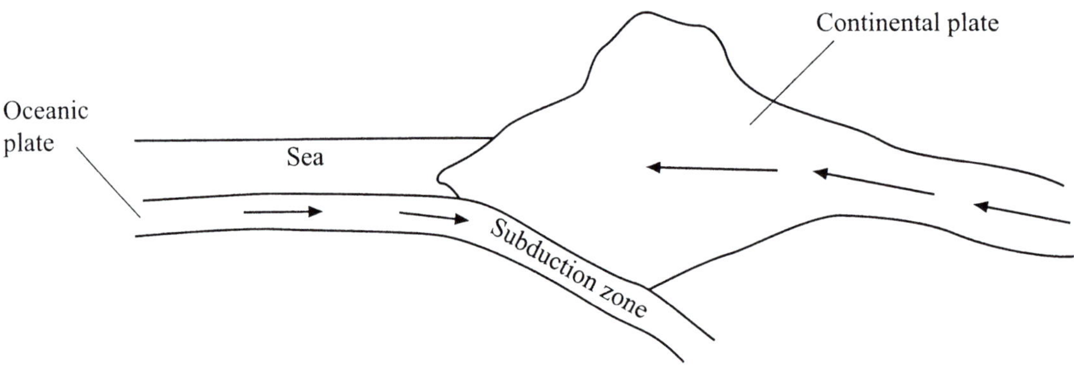

2.1 As the plates move together …

A an oceanic ridge is formed.

B magnetic reversal patterns are formed.

C sea floor spreading takes place.

D the oceanic plate is driven downwards.

2.2 What happens in the subduction zone?

A a large fault develops

B a new sedimentary rock is formed

C new continental crust is formed

D the oceanic plate partially melts to form magma.

2.3 At the plate boundary, the continental plate is forced upwards to form …

A a mountain chain.

B an oceanic ridge.

C new basaltic crust.

D new oceanic crust.

2.4 As the continental plate is forced upwards, the sediments in the plate…

A are folded and metamorphosed.

B are melted.

C become less dense.

D form a basaltic magma.

3 This passage is about the positions of the land masses of South America and Africa.

Match words from the list with each of the spaces **1–4** in the passage.

fossils **plates** **rocks** **shapes**

Some sedimentary deposits on the East Coast of South America and the West Coast of Africa contain similar animal remains that we call ...... **1**......

On these coasts there are also similar patterns of sedimentary ....**2**......

The two land masses have ...... **3**...... which fit quite closely.

These pieces of evidence suggest that the tectonic ....**4**....... on which these land masses lie have moved apart.

Year 11 questions

1 Look at the earthquake zones and volcanoes below: Marks

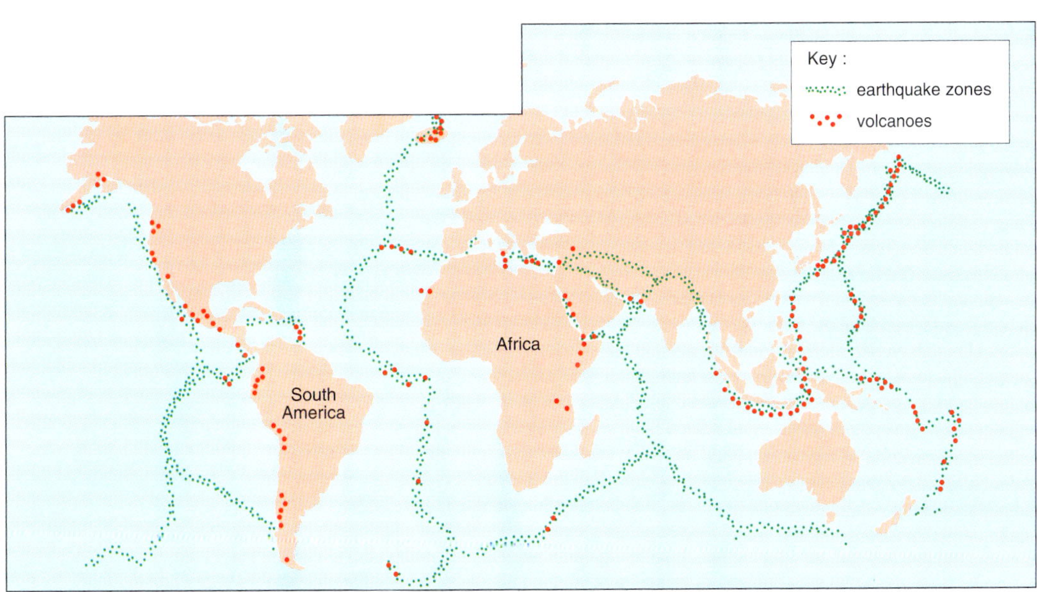

Explain what the map above can tell us about the structure of the Earth.

....

....

(2 marks) 2

Getting the Grades – Earth Materials

Try this question, then compare your answer with the two examples opposite ▶

1 This question is about the way in which crude oil can be converted into useful products.

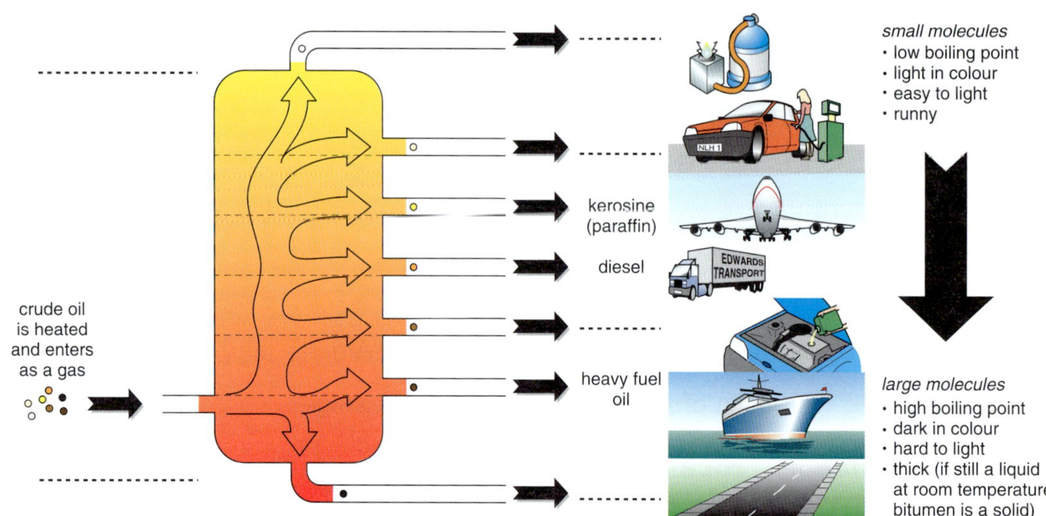

a) Study the diagram of a fractionating column which is shown above. Some of the labels are missing. Choose words from the list below to complete the labels on the diagram:

low temperature, high temperature, petroleum gases, bitumen, petrol, lubricating oil *(3 marks)*

b) Crude oil is a mixture of hydrocarbons.

i Explain what is meant by the term 'mixture'.

.... *(1 mark)*

ii Explain what is meant by the term 'hydrocarbon'.

.... *(2 marks)*

c) Use your own words to explain how the fractionating column separates the different hydrocarbons in crude oil.

....

....

.... *(3 marks)*

d) Some of the larger hydrocarbons are then passed on to a different plant where they undergo a process called **cracking**. This process breaks the molecules up into smaller, more useful and more reactive substances.
One of the possible cracking reactions is shown below:

$$C_{10}H_{22} \longrightarrow C_8H_{18} + C_2H_4$$

decane → octane + ethene

i Why is the octane produced in this way more useful than the decane from which it is made?

....

.... *(1 mark)*

ii The ethene produced is an example of an ***unsaturated*** hydrocarbon. What does the term ***unsaturated*** mean?

....

.... *(1 mark)*

GRADE 'A' ANSWER

1 a) low temperature high temperature ✓
petroleum gases petrol ✓ lubricating oil
bitumen ✓

b) i A mixture is formed when two or more substances are mixed without being chemically combined. ✓

ii A compound containing hydrogen and carbon ✓ only ✓

c) The heat causes the crude oil to vapourise ✓ before it enters the column. Each fraction has a different boiling point. ✓

The candidate has not mentioned different temperatures at the various levels in the column

d) i The more volatile octane will burn better ✓

ii A hydrocarbon whose molecules contain at least one C=C (double) bond. ✓

This shows an excellent definition of an unsaturated hydrocarbon.

10 marks = Grade A answer

Improve your Grades A up to A*

Make sure you can apply your knowledge of evaporation and condensation to explain the process of fractional distillation. At the high temperatures near the bottom of a fractionating column, the smaller hydrocarbons stay as gasses and rise up the column. The larger hydrocarbons condense at the higher temperatures.

GRADE 'C' ANSWER

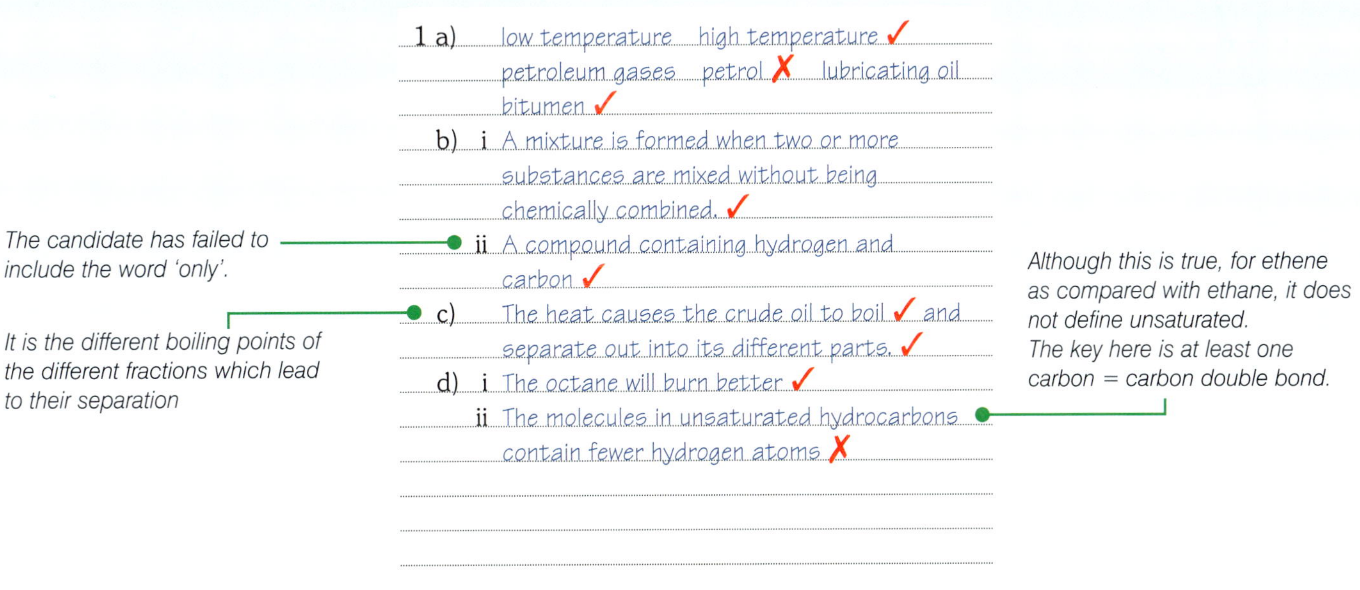

1 a) low temperature high temperature ✓
petroleum gases petrol ✗ lubricating oil
bitumen ✓

b) i A mixture is formed when two or more substances are mixed without being chemically combined. ✓

ii A compound containing hydrogen and carbon ✓

The candidate has failed to include the word 'only'.

c) The heat causes the crude oil to boil ✓ and separate out into its different parts. ✓

It is the different boiling points of the different fractions which lead to their separation

d) i The octane will burn better ✓

ii The molecules in unsaturated hydrocarbons contain fewer hydrogen atoms ✗

Although this is true, for ethene as compared with ethane, it does not define unsaturated. The key here is at least one carbon = carbon double bond.

7 marks = Grade C answer

Improve your Grades C up to B

Make sure you understand the importance of the C=C double bond in unsaturated hydrocarbons. It is the C=C bond that makes alkenes so much more reactive than alkanes. Study and practise drawing diagrams to show alkene molecules undergoing addition polymerisation.

8

ThinkAbout:

1 Which of these factors will increase the rate of a reaction?
   A lowering the temperature
   B increasing the temperature
   C increasing the concentration of solutions
   D decreasing the concentration of solutions.

2 Which gas is given off when limestone reacts with dilute hydrochloric acid?

3 Which gas is given off when magnesium reacts with dilute hydrochloric acid?

4 Name a chemical reaction that takes place:
   a) very slowly
   b) very quickly.

Measuring rates of reaction

We can measure rates of reaction by looking at how quickly products are formed.
We can also measure how quickly reactants are used up.

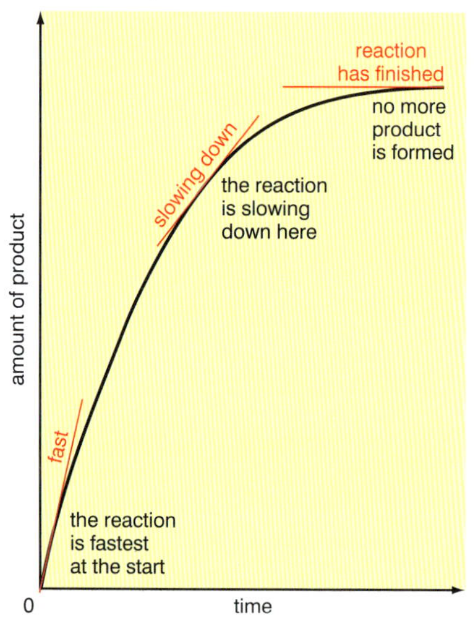

amount of reactant

time/s

Collision theory

We explain rates of reaction using the **collision theory**.

> Particles must collide, with enough energy, before a reaction can occur.

This minimum amount of energy is called the **activation energy**.

Effect of surface area

> Rates of reaction are increased by increasing the **surface area** (using small pieces) of solids.

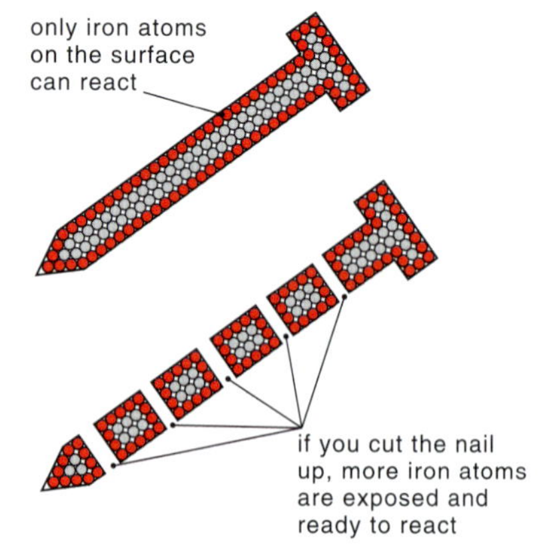

Answers:

1 B and C **2** carbon dioxide **3** hydrogen **4** a) e.g. iron rusting/concrete setting b) e.g. dynamite exploding / acid neutralising an alkali

Effect of concentration

Rates of reaction are increased by increasing the **concentration** of solutions.

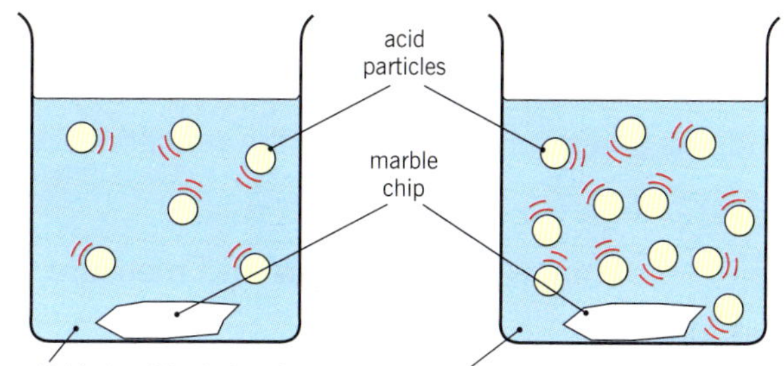

When we increase the concentration (or pressure in gas reactions), there are more particles in the same space so particles collide more often.

Take care:
When explaining the effect of concentration, don't just say that there are more particles – explain that there are more particles ***in a given volume*** and therefore more collisions ***in a given time***.

Rates of reaction are increased by increasing the **pressure** of gases.

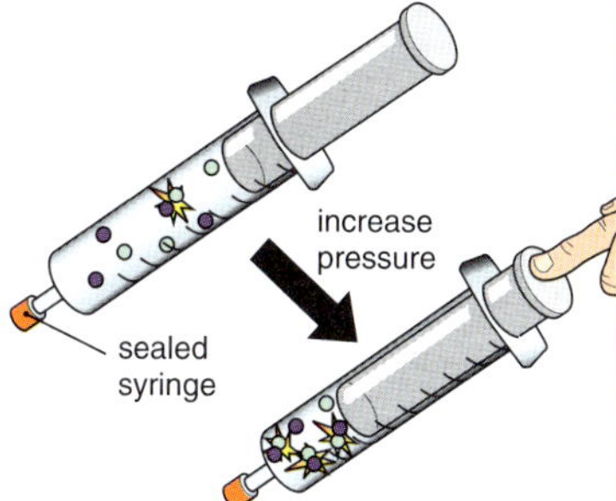

Effect of temperature

Rates of reaction are increased by increasing the **temperature**.

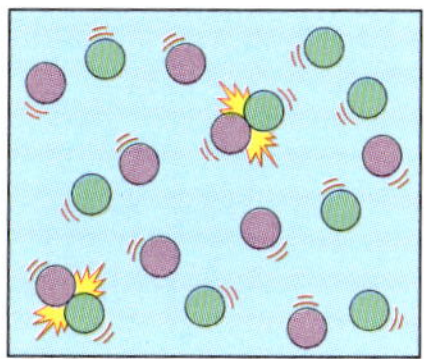
Reaction at 30 °C

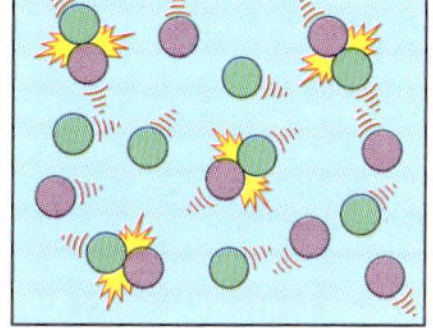
Reaction at 40 °C

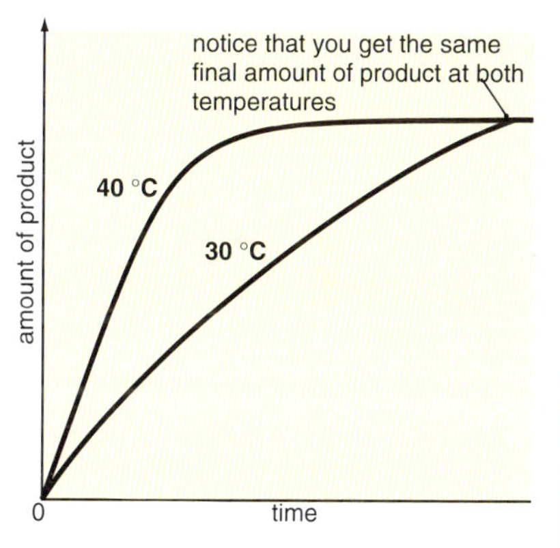

When we increase the temperature, the reacting particles gain more energy:

- They move around faster, so collisions are **more frequent**.
- The collisions are also **more energetic,** so are more likely to produce a reaction (more reacting particles will have energy that exceeds the **activation energy** for the reaction).

Catalysts

Rates of reaction are increased by using a **catalyst.** (That is, if you can find one for a particular reaction, as different reactions need different catalysts.)

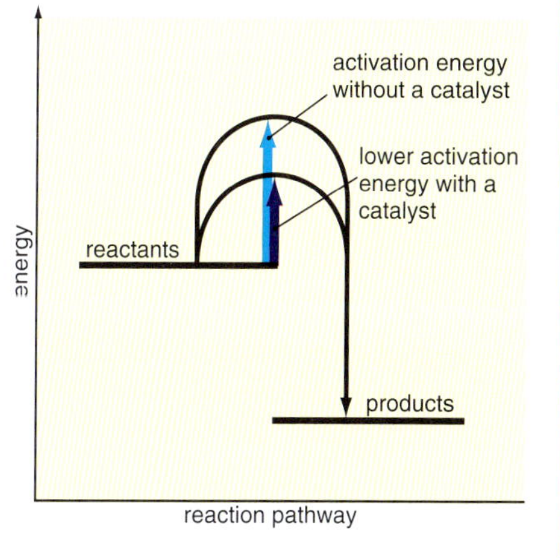

A catalyst can be used over and over again as it is not chemically changed itself at the end of the reaction.

More in ***Chemistry for You***, pages 199–211.

Examination Questions – Rates of reaction

Year 11 questions

1 Some students investigate the rate of the reaction between magnesium and dilute hydrochloric acid.

They use 0.1 g of magnesium **ribbon** and measure the volume of hydrogen produced at 30 second intervals.

The reaction ends when all the magnesium is used up.

The results are shown on the graph.

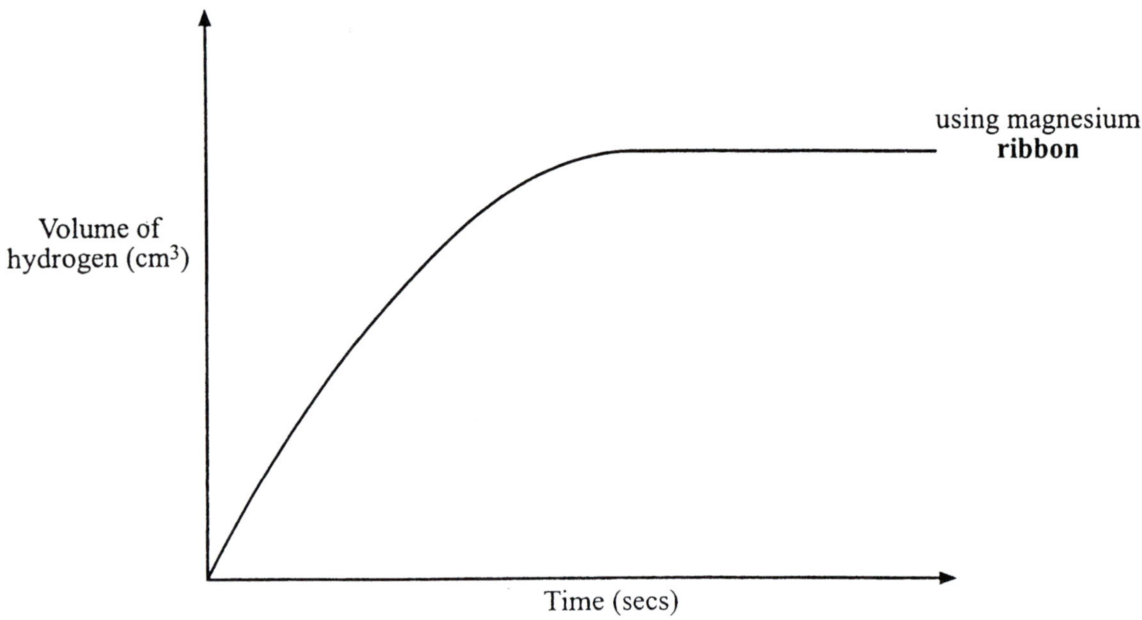

The students do the experiment again. This time they use the same volume of the same acid but with 0.1 g of magnesium **powder**.

Marks

a) On the graph above, sketch the curve you would expect the students to obtain.

(2 marks)

b) The rate of reaction between magnesium and hydrochloric acid is greater if the concentration of the acid is increased.

Explain why, in terms of particles.

....

....

....

(2 marks)

c) When the reaction is finished, a solution of magnesium chloride is left behind.
Write a word equation for the reaction between magnesium and hydrochloric acid.

.... + ... ⟶ .... + ...

(2 marks) 6

2 Calcium carbonate reacts with dilute nitric acid to produce carbon dioxide.

$$CaCO_3 + 2HNO_3 \rightarrow Ca(NO_3)_2 + H_2O + CO_2$$

A 10 g lump of calcium carbonate was reacted with 20 cm^3 of dilute nitric acid. When the reaction was finished, some of the calcium carbonate was left unreacted. The graph shows the volume of carbon dioxide made in each minute for sixteen minutes.

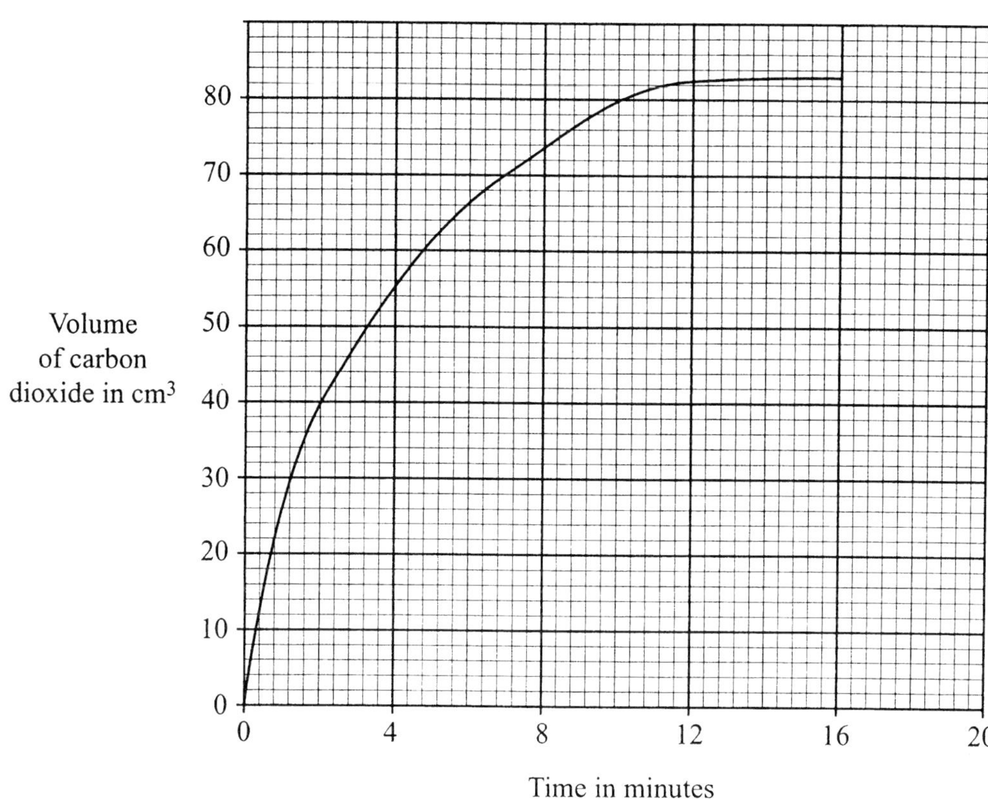

Marks

a) The volume of the carbon dioxide made each minute decreases until it remains steady at 83 cm^3
Explain why.

....

....

....

....

(2 marks)

b) Draw a line, on the axes above, for an experiment where 20 cm^3 of the same dilute nitric acid was reacted with 10 g of powdered calcium carbonate.

(2 marks)

c) Give **one** way of changing the rate of this reaction (other than using powdered calcium carbonate).

....

....

....

(1 mark)

5

9

▶ ThinkAbout:

1 How are enzymes used in your digestive system?
2 Are the conditions in your stomach acidic, alkaline or neutral?
3 At which temperature are the enzymes in your body likely to work best?
A 0 °C   B 20 °C   C 40 °C   D 60 °C
4 How could you test that the gas given off during fermentation is carbon dioxide?

▶ How enzymes work

The chemical reactions in living cells are catalysed by **enzymes**.

Enzymes are called **biological catalysts**.
They are large **protein** molecules.

Their special complex shapes match the molecules they help to react.

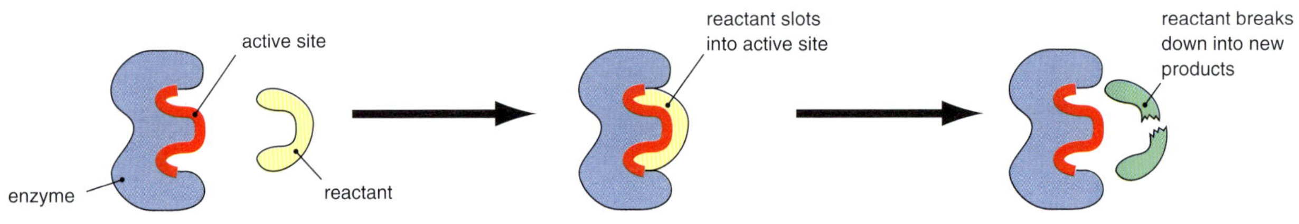

D

▶ Optimum conditions

Enzymes work best at around 40 °C (their **optimum temperature**).
However, over about 45 °C they are damaged and their special shape is changed.
They are **denatured** and become much less effective.

Each enzyme also works best at a particular pH value (called its **optimum pH**).

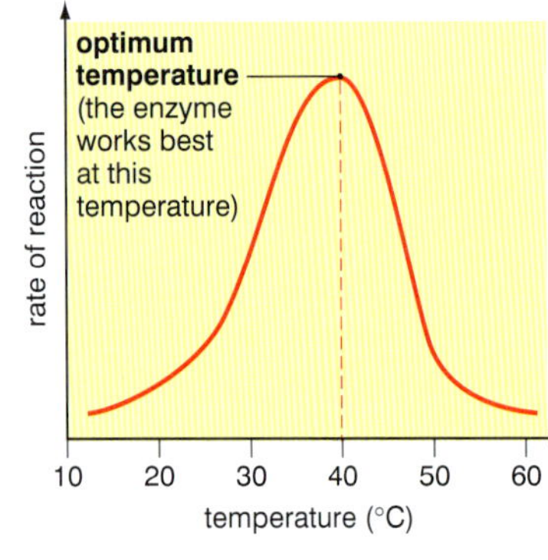

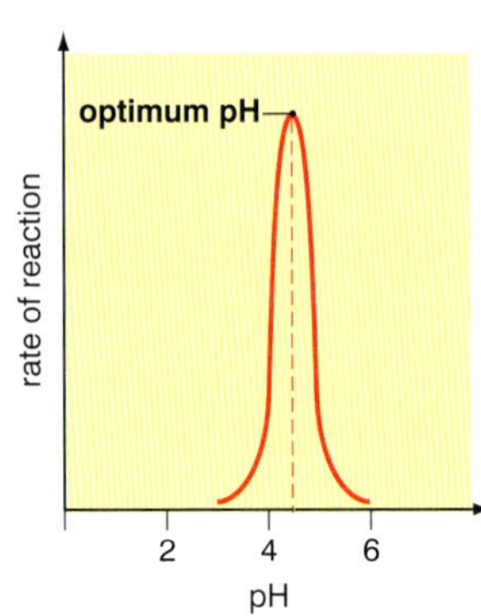

Answers:
1 to break down large food molecules **2** acidic **3** C, 40 °C
4 bubble the gas into limewater which will turn milky

Fermentation

Fermentation is the reaction in which yeast cells convert sugar (glucose) into alcohol (ethanol) and carbon dioxide gas:

$$\text{sugar (glucose)} \xrightarrow{\text{enzymes in yeast}} \text{alcohol (ethanol)} + \text{carbon dioxide}$$

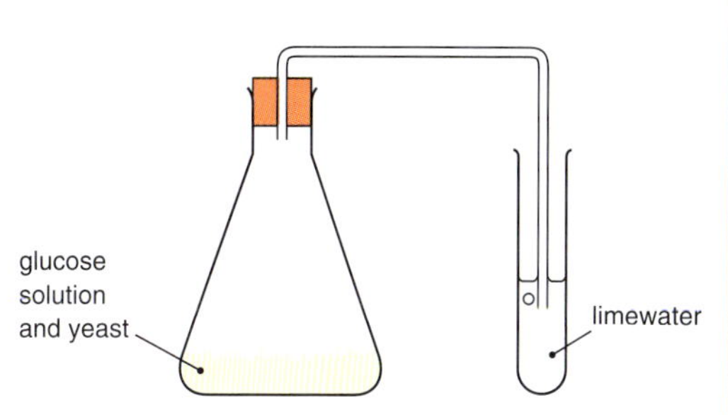

The reaction is catalysed by enzymes in the yeast cells, in the absence of oxygen.

We use fermentation to make:

- the alcohol in wine and beer
- the bubbles (of carbon dioxide) that make bread dough rise.

Other uses of enzymes

Enzymes can save energy costs in industry because reactions can take place at relatively low temperatures. Researchers are finding more and more uses.
For example, enzymes are used:

- in biological washing powders and liquids to break down stains
- in some baby foods to 'pre-digest' proteins
- to change starch syrup into sugar syrup
- to convert glucose into the less fattening sugar called fructose
- to make yoghurt (changing lactose, a sugar, in milk into lactic acid).

Techniques in biotechnology

H

Scientists have had to find ways to use enzymes to greatest effect and have found how to:

- keep enzymes active for longer periods
- immobilise the enzymes by trapping them in an inert support or on carrier beads (of calcium alginate).

These techniques make the process of making the new substance **continuous**, rather than the **batch process** used in traditional enzyme reactions, such as brewing.

Take care:

- Enzymes are molecules found ***in*** living things.
- They are not living things themselves, so they ***cannot*** be killed!

More in ***Chemistry for You***, pages 212–19.

Examination Questions – Enzymes

Year 11 questions

Marks

1 Living cells are used to make beer and yoghurt.

a) Complete each sentence by using the correct words from the box.

alcohol	**fructose**	**lactic acid**	**milk sugar**
oxygen	**protein**	**starch**	**sugar**

In beer-making, yeast converts .... into carbon dioxide and ....

In yoghurt-making, bacteria convert .... into ....

(4 marks)

b) Describe the test for carbon dioxide.

....

....

....

(2 marks) 6

2 We can use yeast to change sugar into alcohol and carbon dioxide. This process is called fermentation.

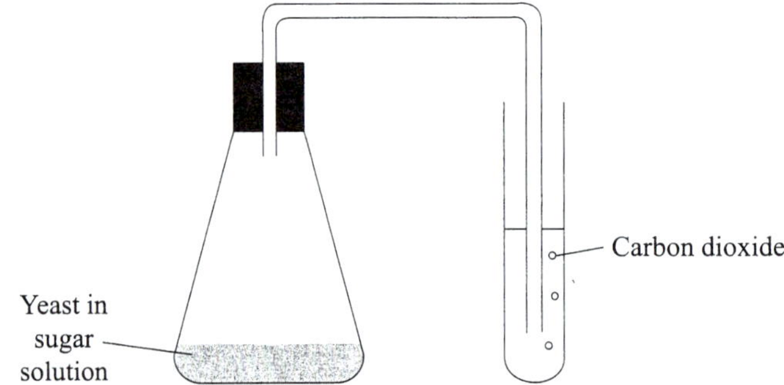

a) Complete the sentences by choosing the correct words from the box.

bread	**cheese**	**wine**	**yoghurt**

Alcohol produced in this way is used in making ....

Carbon dioxide produced by fermentation can be used to make .... rise.

(2 marks)

b) Three test tubes were set up, as shown below. The temperature was kept at 15°C.

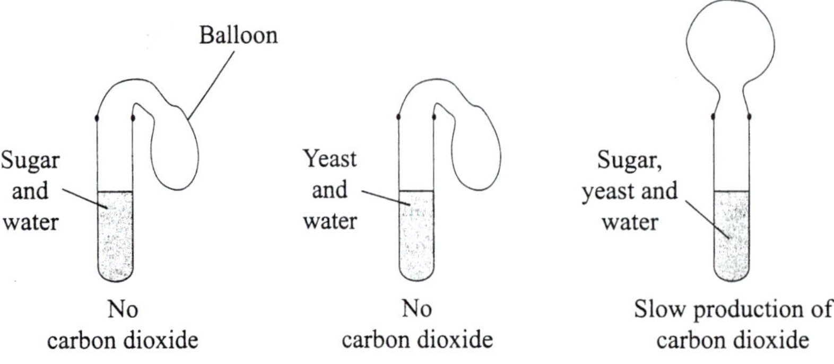

Marks

i Give **one** advantage of using enzymes in chemical reactions.

(1 mark)

ii Give **one** disadvantage of using enzymes in chemical reactions.

(1 mark) 4

3 The diagram shows how a beer called Newcastle Brown Ale is made.

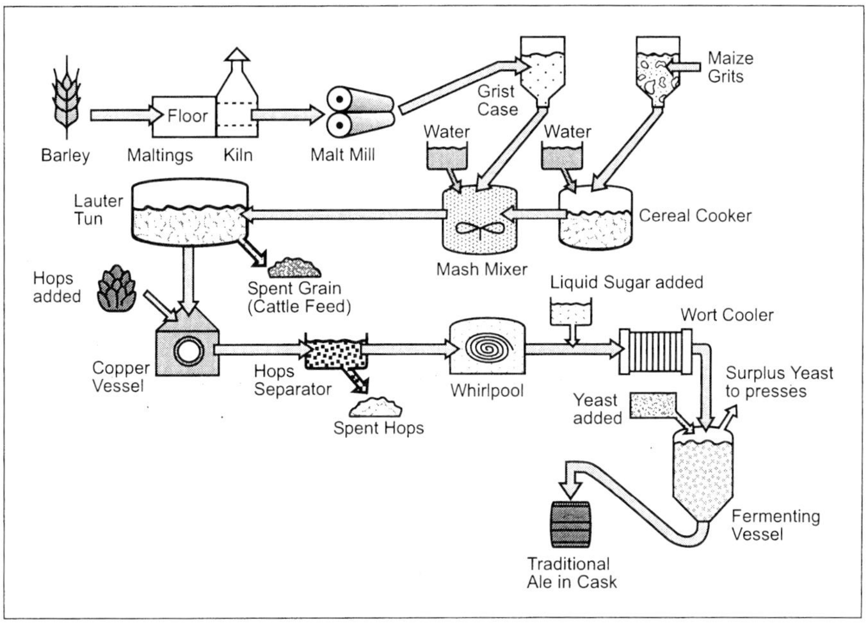

a) Use the diagram to help you to name four of the raw materials used to make this beer.

1. .... 2. ....

3. .... 4. ....

(2 marks)

b) In the Mash Mixer sugars are formed. The reaction is helped by an enzyme.
How does the enzyme help the reaction?

(1 mark)

c) In the fermenting vessel sugars are changed into two products.
One of these is alcohol (ethanol). Name the other product.

(1 mark)

d) The fermenting vessel is cooled using cold water because the fermentation reaction gives out heat.

i What name is given to reactions that give out heat?

(1 mark)

ii A solution of sugar containing enzymes must not be allowed to become too hot.
Explain why.

(1 mark) 6

10

ThinkAbout:

1. You are holding the bottom of a beaker containing two solutions that react together in an exothermic reaction. What do you feel?
2. In a reversible reaction, the forward reaction gives out 150 kJ mol^{-1} of energy. What energy do you think the reverse reaction will take in?
3. Where do we get the energy our bodies need to survive?
4. Do you think we need to put energy into a compound to break its bonds, or do you think energy will be given out in this process?

Exothermic and endothermic reactions

D

Reactions that give out energy, often as heat, are called **exothermic**.
The temperature of the surroundings rises.

Reactions that take in energy are called **endothermic**. The temperature of the surroundings falls.

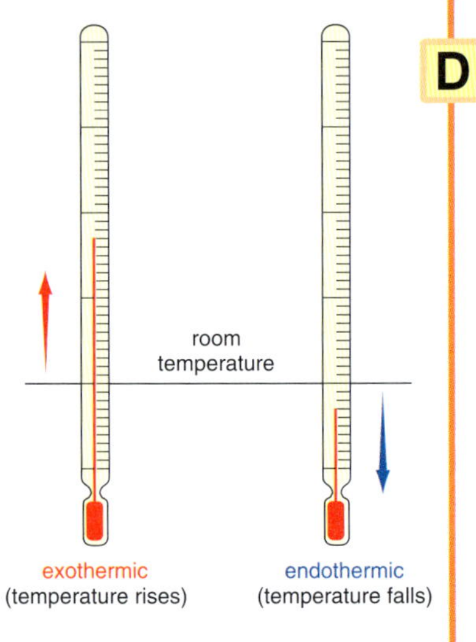

Energy transfer in reversible reactions

In a reversible reaction:

- If the forward reaction is exothermic, the reverse reaction is endothermic.
- If the forward reaction is endothermic, the reverse reaction is exothermic.

In a reversible reaction, the amount of energy given out or taken in will be equal for the forward and reverse reactions.

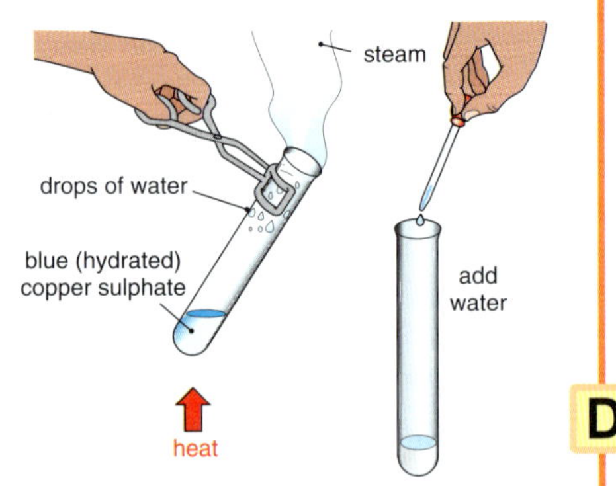

D

An example is when we heat blue hydrated copper sulphate crystals:

hydrated copper sulphate (+ ***heat energy***) $\rightleftharpoons$ anhydrous copper sulphate + water
blue crystals ***white powder***

Answers: **1** It will feel warm/hot. **2** 150 kJ mol^{-1} **3** food **4** put energy in

Energy level diagrams

We can show energy changes in chemical reactions on an energy level diagram.

ΔH is the symbol for the energy change in a reaction.

ΔH is negative for an **exothermic** reaction.

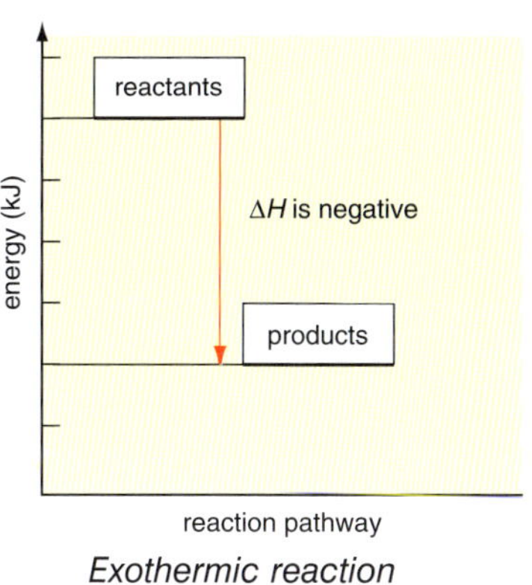

Exothermic reaction

ΔH is positive for an **endothermic** reaction.

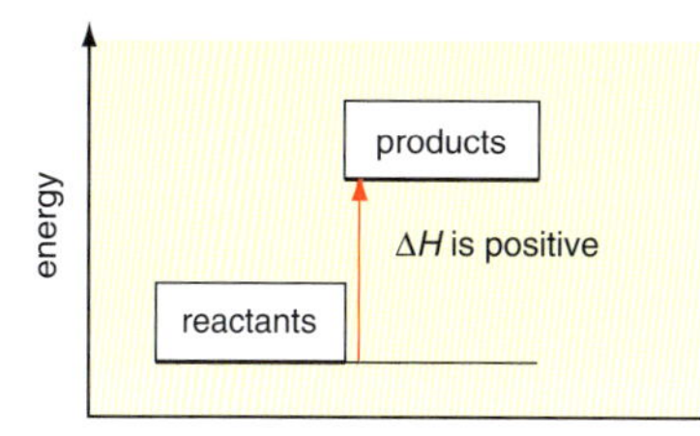

Endothermic reaction

D H

Bond energies

Breaking bonds requires energy. It is an **endothermic** process.

Making new bonds gives out energy. It is an **exothermic** process.

- Bond energies are a measure of the ***strength*** of a bond.
- We can use bond energies to work out an approximate value of ΔH for a reaction.
- If the energy given out when new bonds form is ***greater than*** the energy needed to break the existing bonds, then the reaction is exothermic.
- If the energy given out when new bonds form is ***less than*** the energy needed to break the existing bonds, then the reaction is endothermic.

Example

Calculate the approximate energy change accompanying the reaction between hydrogen and chlorine to make hydrogen chloride:

$$H_2 + Cl_2 \longrightarrow 2HCl$$

(Bond energy values are: H—H = 436 kJ mol^{-1}, Cl—Cl = 242 kJ mol^{-1}, H—Cl = 431 kJ mol^{-1})

Bonds broken:

$+[1 \times (\text{H—H})] + [1 \times (\text{Cl—Cl})]$

$= +(436 + 242)$

$= +678$ kJ mol^{-1}

Bonds made:

$-(2 \times \text{H—Cl})$

$= -(2 \times 431)$

$= -862$ kJ mol^{-1}

Adding these two up to get the overall energy change we get:

$(+678) + (-862)$

$=$ **-184 kJ mol^{-1}**

D H

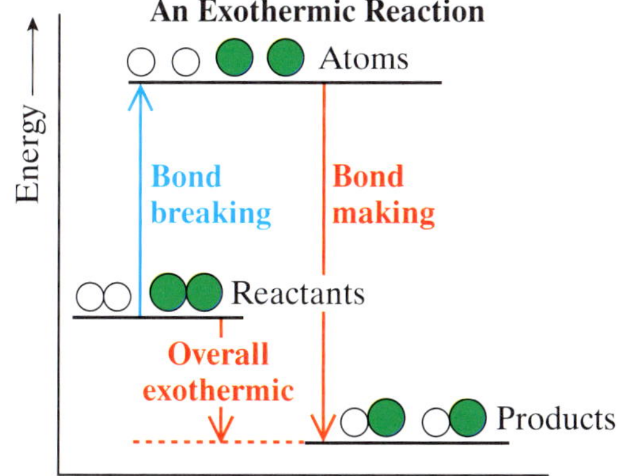

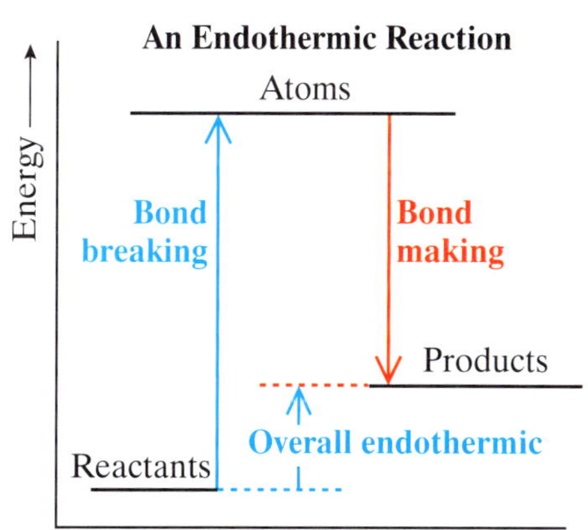

More in ***Chemistry for You***, pages 190–97.

Examination Questions – Energy transfer

Year 11 questions

1 This question is about the reaction between magnesium and hydrochloric acid. Marks

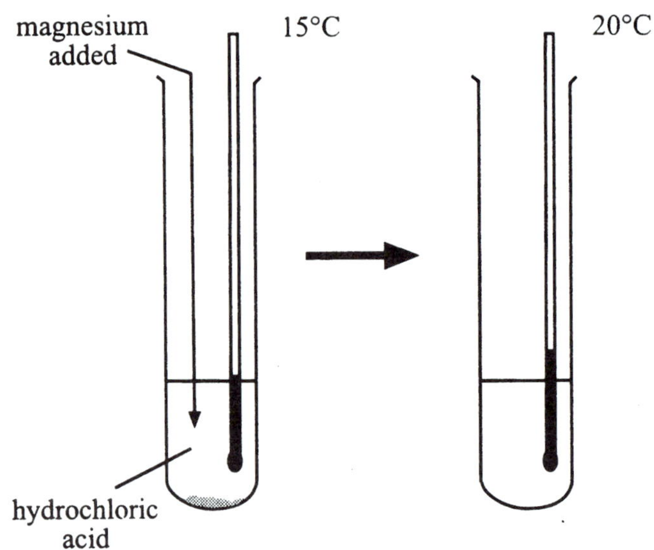

Choose words from the list to complete the sentence below.

endothermic **exothermic** **oxidation**

obtained from **released as light to** **released as heat to**

The reaction between magnesium and hydrochloric acid is an ....

reaction because energy is .... the surroundings.

(2 marks) 2

2 Hydrogen will combine with chlorine to produce hydrogen chloride.

The reaction can be represented by this equation.

$$H_2 + Cl_2 \longrightarrow 2HCl$$

$$H{-}H + Cl{-}Cl \longrightarrow 2H{-}Cl$$

a) Show, by calculation, that this reaction is exothermic.
(All your working should be shown).

Bond	Energy needed to break bonds or released when bonds are formed (kJ per formula mass)
H—H	436
Cl—Cl	240
H—Cl	431

Marks

....

....

....

....

....

(3 marks)

b) At room temperature a piece of magnesium ribbon does not burn in chlorine. However, if we light the magnesium ribbon first, then place it in chlorine, it burns with a powerful, white flame.

This exothermic reaction can be represented by a word equation.

magnesium + chlorine ⟶ magnesium chloride

Sketch an energy level diagram for the reaction and show on the diagram, the nett energy released.

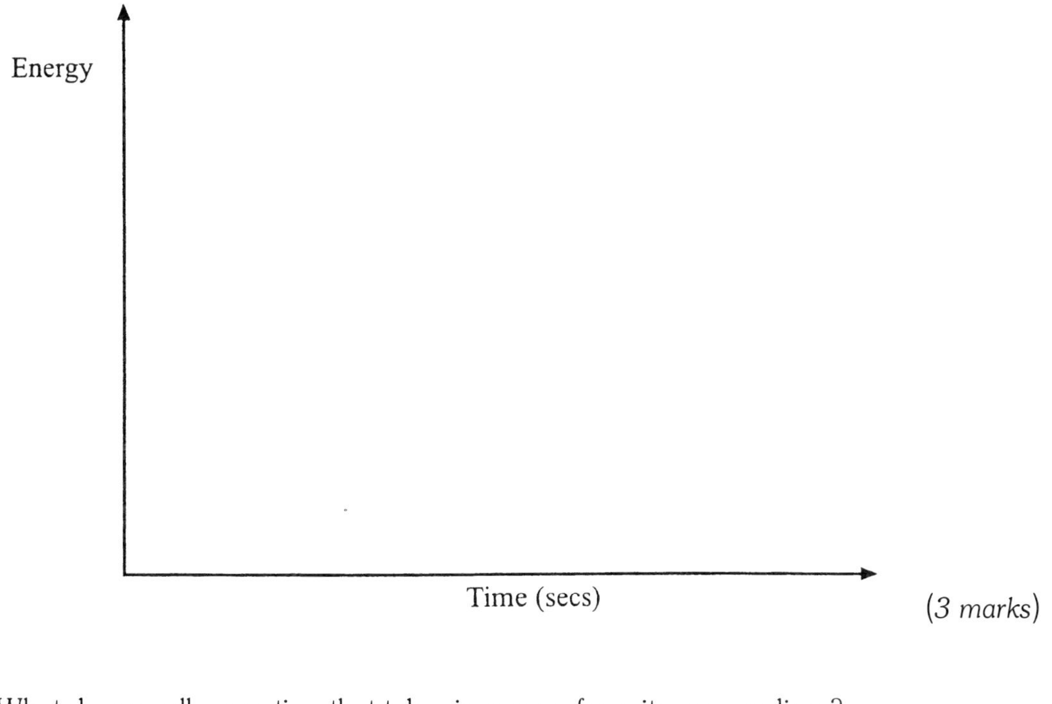

(3 marks)

c) What do we call a reaction that takes in energy from its surroundings?

....

(1 mark)

d) Look at the reaction below (the letters are not chemical symbols):

$$X + Y \longrightarrow Z$$

This reaction gives out 125 kJ mol^{-1}

What will be the energy change when Z decomposes to form X and Y?
Will this energy be given out or taken in?

....

(2 marks) 9

11

ThinkAbout:

1 What is the chemical formula of ammonia?
2 What is the main gas (with the highest percentage) in the air?
3 Name the reactive gas in the air.
4 What do plants make with the nitrogen they take in from fertilisers?

Making ammonia – The Haber process

D

Although almost 80% of the air is nitrogen gas, most plants can't use this directly to help them grow. So we add nitrogen-based **fertilisers** to the soil.
These are soluble compounds that can be absorbed through the roots of a plant.
However, these fertilisers can cause pollution in our water supplies and in rivers.

Nitrogen is converted to ammonia (NH_3) in the **Haber process**:

$$\text{nitrogen} + \text{hydrogen} \rightleftharpoons \text{ammonia}$$
$$N_2(g) + 3H_2(g) \rightleftharpoons 2NH_3(g)$$

- The catalyst used is iron.
- The temperature is about 450 °C.
- The pressure is about 200 atmospheres.

These conditions are chosen to give a reasonable yield of ammonia as quickly as possible.
The ammonia gas is cooled down. It condenses to a liquid that is collected.

Any unreacted nitrogen and hydrogen are recycled to the start of the process.

Facts about the Haber process

Raw materials
Air (for nitrogen)
Natural gas (to make hydrogen)
Steam (to make hydrogen and to generate high pressures)

Conditions
Temperature : about 450 °C
Pressure : about 200 atmospheres
Catalyst : mainly iron

The Haber process

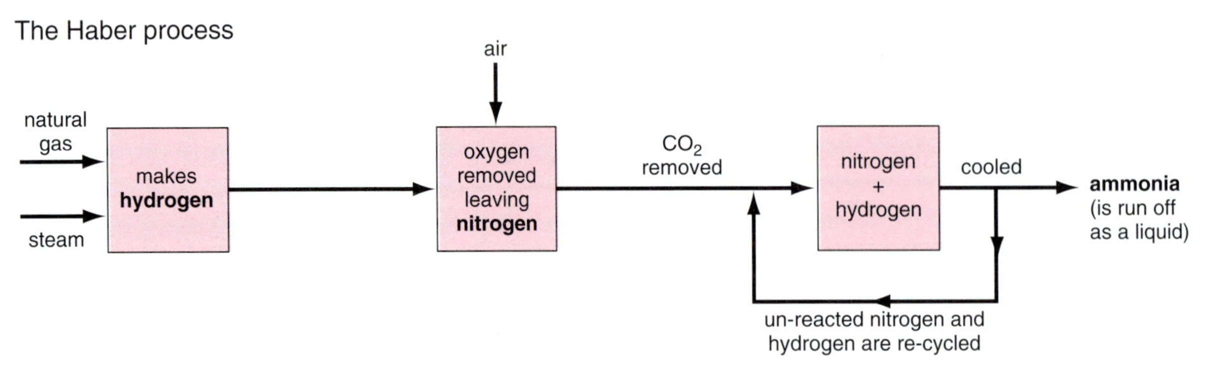

Answers: 1 NH_3 2 nitrogen 3 oxygen 4 proteins

Making nitric acid and ammonium nitrate fertiliser

D

Some of the ammonia from the Haber process is used to make **nitric acid** (HNO_3). Ammonia is oxidised to **nitrogen monoxide** and water, by passing it over a hot platinum catalyst:

$$\text{ammonia} + \text{oxygen} \rightleftharpoons \text{nitrogen monoxide} + \text{water}$$

This nitrogen monoxide is then cooled down and reacted with more oxygen and water, to make the **nitric acid**:

$$\text{nitrogen monoxide} + \text{oxygen} \rightleftharpoons \text{nitrogen dioxide}$$

$$\text{nitrogen dioxide} + \text{oxygen} + \text{water} \longrightarrow \text{nitric acid}$$

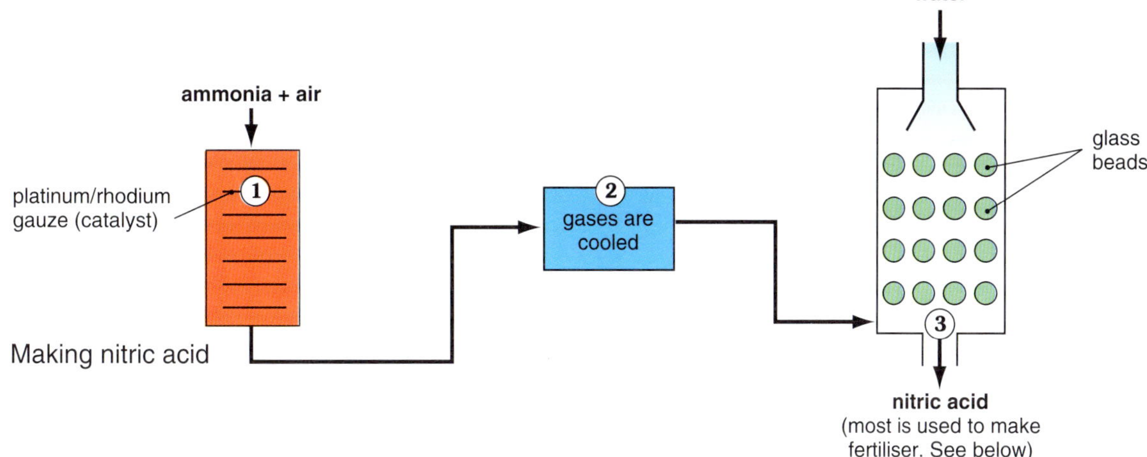

Making nitric acid

We can then use the neutralisation between nitric acid and more ammonia to make the fertiliser called **ammonium nitrate** (NH_4NO_3):

$$NH_3(aq) + HNO_3(aq) \longrightarrow NH_4NO_3(aq)$$

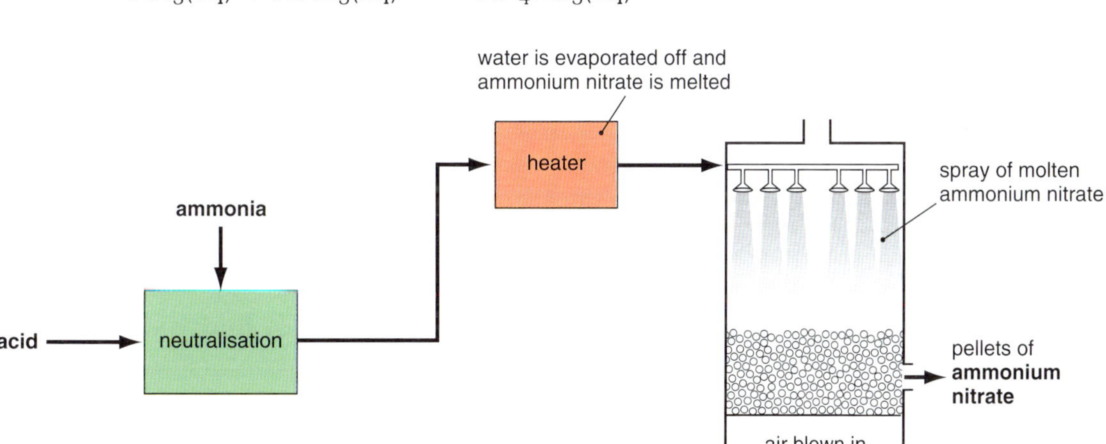

Making ammonium nitrate

Take care:

- Most positive ions are formed by metals e.g. Mg^{2+}.
- The ammonium ion, NH_4^+, is an exception.

More in ***Chemistry for You***, pages 127–34 and 242–251.

Examination Questions – Useful products from air

Year 11 questions

1 Nitric acid is made from ammonia, NH_3.

The first stage in this process can be shown in a flow diagram.

Look at the flow diagram below.

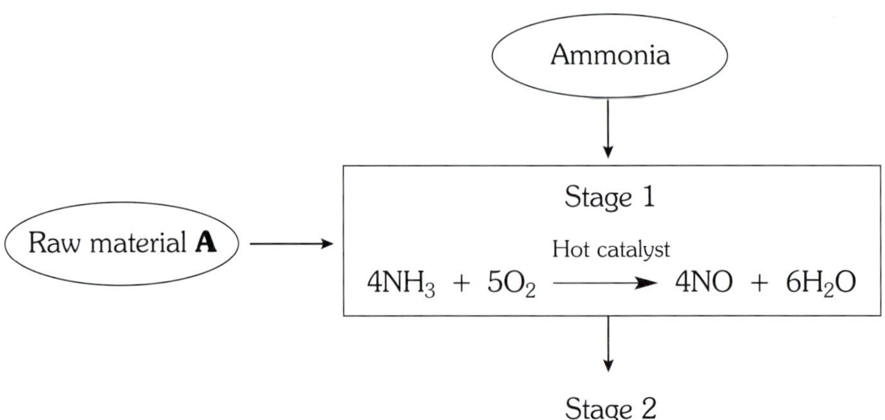

a) Name raw material **A** Marks

....

(*1 mark*)

b) Draw a ring around:

i the name of the catalyst used in stage 1;

gold **iron** **mercury** **platinum** (*1 mark*)

ii the word which best describes this reaction.

decomposition **displacement** **neutralisation** **oxidation**

c) Nitric acid can be neutralised by alkalis to make salts. (*1 mark*)

i The salt called potassium nitrate can be made from nitric acid.

Complete the word equation for this neutralisation reaction.

Choose the correct substances from the box.

hydrogen	**oxygen**	**potassium chloride**	**potassium hydroxide**	**water**

nitric acid + ... → potassium nitrate + ...

(*2 marks*)

ii Ammonium nitrate is another salt made from nitric acid.

Which one of the following is the main use of ammonium nitrate?

Draw a ring around your answer.

dye **fertiliser** **plastic** **fuel** (*1 mark*)

iii Complete this sentence by choosing the correct ion from the box.

H^+	NH_4^+	NO_3^-	O^{2-}	OH^-

The ion that makes solutions acidic is .... (*1 mark*) 7

2 The diagram shows the final stages in the manufacture of ammonia.

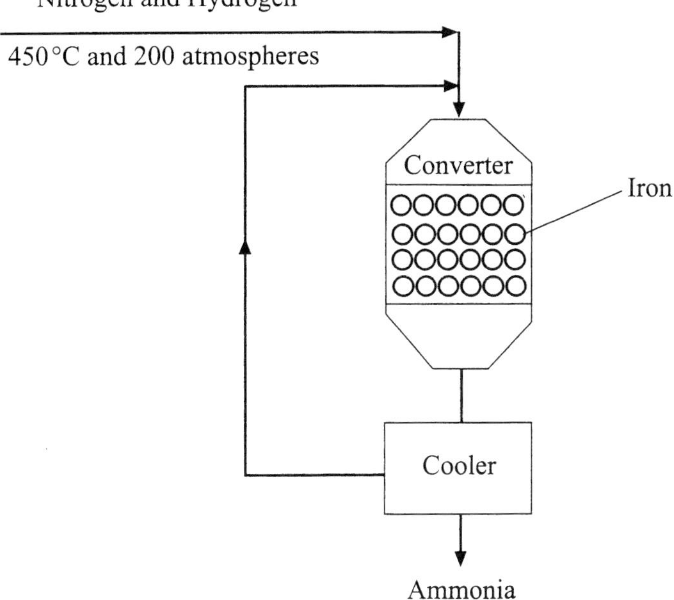

Marks

a) Why is iron used in the converter?

....

....

(1 mark)

b) Write the word equation for the reaction in the converter.

.... + ... ⇌ ....

(1 mark)

c) The yield of ammonia is only about 15%.

i Why can the yield not be 100%?

....

....

(1 mark)

ii Describe what happens to the mixture of gases after it leaves the converter.

....

....

....

(2 marks)

d) i Name the raw material used to obtain nitrogen for the process.

....

(1 mark)

ii Complete this sentence.

Natural gas is the raw material for the .... used in the process.

(1 mark) 7

12

Reversible ⇌ Reactions

ThinkAbout:

1 What is the main difference between a physical change and a reversible chemical change?

2 What do you see if you add too much acid to an alkaline solution containing universal indicator, and then add too much alkali?

3 a) How can you test for the presence of water using anhydrous copper sulphate?
b) Give another chemical test for the presence of water.
c) How could you show that the liquid was pure water?

D

Examples of reversible reactions

Some reactions are **reversible**.
The reactants form the products, but the products can also react together to re-form the reactants:

reactants $\rightleftharpoons$ products

- The test for water (white anhydrous copper sulphate turns blue) is a reversible reaction.
- The breakdown and formation of ammonium chloride is reversible:

ammonium chloride $\rightleftharpoons$ ammonia + hydrogen chloride

$NH_4Cl(s) \rightleftharpoons NH_3(g) + HCl(g)$

a white solid ***colourless gases***

When the white ammonium chloride powder is heated it decomposes. It gives off ammonia and hydrogen chloride gases. On the cool part of the test tube, the gases re-combine to form the white solid again.

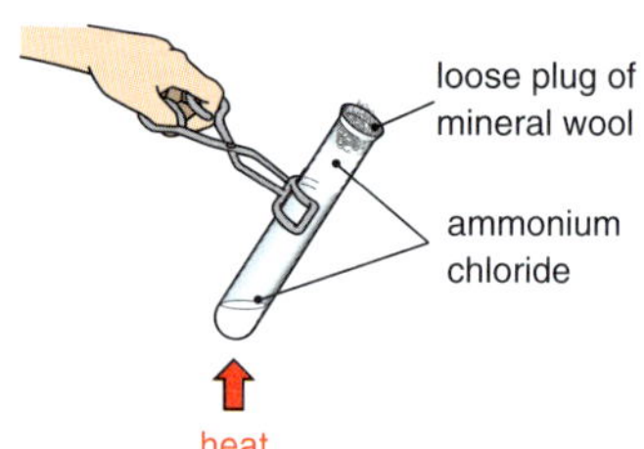

D H

Dynamic equilibrium

When a reaction is in a state of **dynamic equilibrium,** the forward rate is the same as the reverse rate of reaction.

Therefore there appears to be no change in the quantities of substances present in the reacting mixture.

e.g. $A + B \rightleftharpoons C + D$

All four substances (A, B, C and D) will be present in fixed proportions once equilibrium has been reached.

Answers:

1 New substances are formed in reversible chemical changes but not in physical changes.
2 purple → red → purple again
3 a) It turns blue if water is present. b) Blue cobalt chloride turns pink. c) It would boil at 100 °C.

Affecting the position of equilibrium D 

The position of equilibrium shifts to ***oppose*** whatever change we introduce to the system.

The various factors are shown below:

Changing concentration

- ***Increasing*** the concentration of one of the substances in the equilibrium mixture moves the position of equilibrium to favour the ***opposite side***.

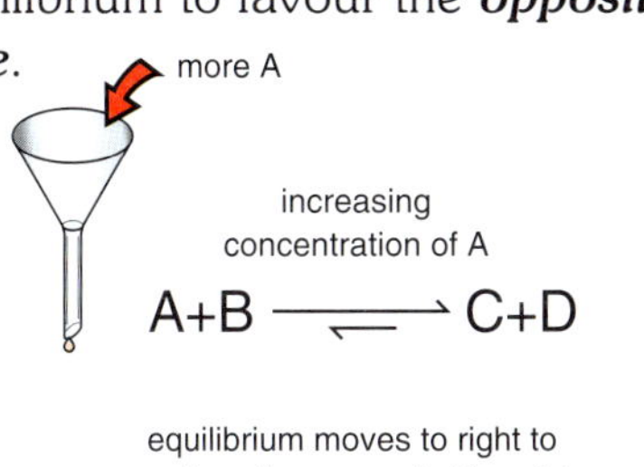

D H

Effect of temperature

- ***Increasing*** the temperature shifts the position of equilibrium to favour the ***endothermic reaction***.
- ***Decreasing*** the temperature shifts the position of equilibrium to favour the ***exothermic reaction***.

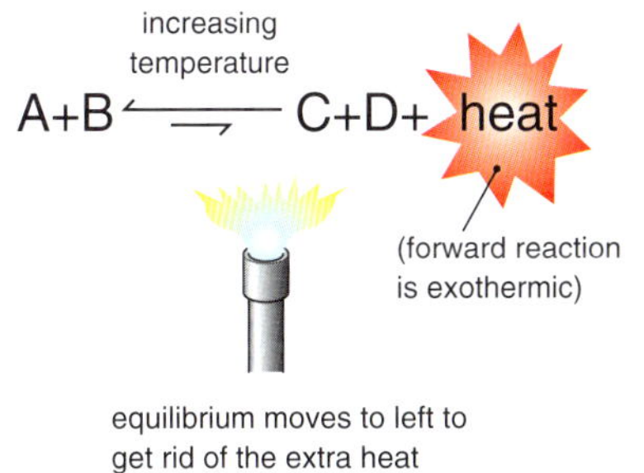

D H

Effect of pressure

In reactions involving different numbers of gas molecules on either side of the equation:

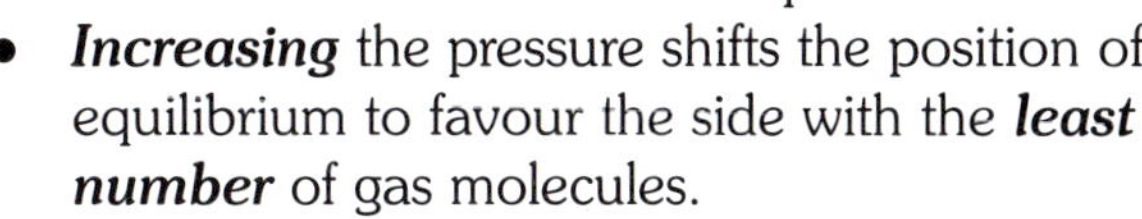

- ***Increasing*** the pressure shifts the position of equilibrium to favour the side with the ***least number*** of gas molecules.

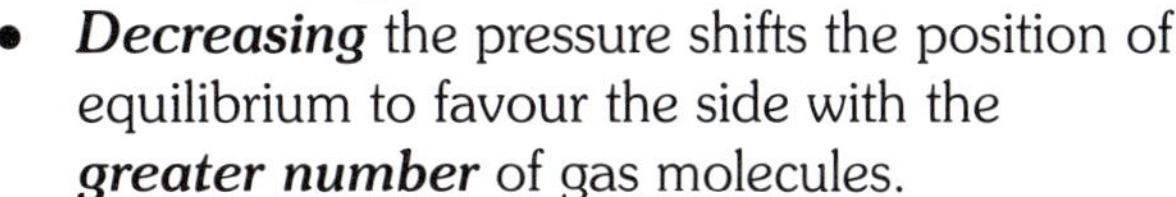

- ***Decreasing*** the pressure shifts the position of equilibrium to favour the side with the ***greater number*** of gas molecules.

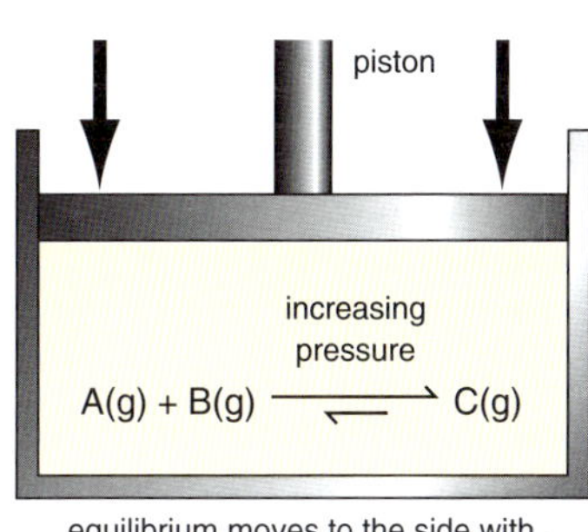

D H

Take care:

- Reversible reactions in industry are not always carried out at the highest possible temperature.
- If a high temperature favours the reactants, a temperature is chosen that is a compromise between a lower yield and a faster rate of reaction.

Reversible reactions in industry

In industrial processes that involve reversible reactions, chemists have to balance the need for a reasonable yield with the need for a fast rate of reaction. For example, in the **Haber process**:

$$N_2(g) + 3H_2(g) \rightleftharpoons 2NH_3(g) \quad \Delta H = -92\ \text{kJ mol}^{-1} \text{ (exothermic in forward direction)}$$

D H

- A low temperature favours a high yield of ammonia, but at a slow rate. So a temperature of 450 °C is chosen as a compromise between yield and rate.
- Iron is used as a catalyst to speed up the rate of reaction. But because it speeds up both the forward and reverse reaction, it doesn't affect the yield of ammonia.

A **catalyst** speeds up the ***rate*** at which we reach equilibrium, but does not affect the position of equilibrium.

More in ***Chemistry for You***, pages 232–41.

Examination Questions – Reversible reactions

Year 11 questions

1 A student heated some blue copper sulphate crystals. The crystals turned into white anhydrous copper sulphate.

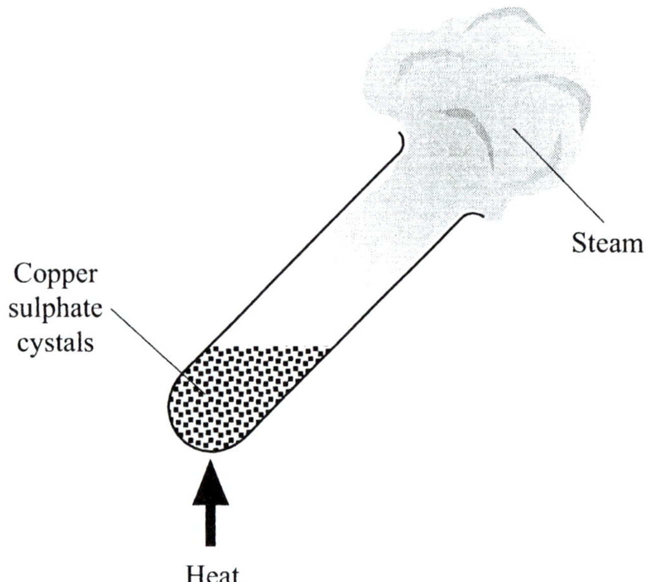

Marks

a) The blue copper sulphate had to be heated to change it into white copper sulphate.

State whether the reaction was exothermic or endothermic.

....

Explain your answer.

....

....

(1 mark)

b) The word equation for this reaction is shown below.

hydrated copper sulphate (blue)	[+ heat energy]	$\rightleftharpoons$	anhydrous copper sulphate (white)	+	water

i What does the symbol $\rightleftharpoons$ tell you about this reaction?

....

(1 mark)

ii How could the student turn the white powder back to blue?

....

(1 mark) 3

2 This question is about the reaction between nitrogen and hydrogen to make the gas ammonia. Look carefully at the equation below

$$N_2(g) + 3H_2(g) \overset{\text{Iron catalyst}}{\rightleftharpoons} 2NH_3(g) \quad \Delta H = -92\ kJmol^{-1}$$

The reaction is a dynamic equilibrium.

a) What symbol shown above is used to represent a dynamic equilibrium? Marks

....

(1 mark)

The forward reaction in this equilibrium is exothermic.

b) How can you tell that the reaction above is exothermic?

....

(1 mark)

c) Changing conditions such as temperature and pressure can have an effect on the position of the equilibrium and therefore the yield of ammonia.

i What effect will an increase in pressure have upon the position of the equilibrium?

....

....

(1 mark)

ii How will an increase in pressure affect the yield of ammonia?

....

(1 mark)

iii How will an increase in temperature affect the yield of ammonia?

....

....

(2 marks)

In the industrial process the reaction is performed at a temperature between 400 °C and 450 °C.

d) Explain why this temperature is a compromise?

....

....

(2 marks)

e) Particles of finely divided iron are used as a catalyst for this process. Why does a catalyst help?

....

....

(2 marks) 10

13 Chemical calculations

mass ÷ moles

$1 \times A_r$ of Ca = 40

no. of moles = $\frac{\text{mass}}{\text{R.F.M.}}$

Relative formula mass of NO_2

Chemists use a large number (6.02×10^{23}) called the **mole** when 'counting' atoms by weighing them out. They know the relative masses of each element. This is called the relative atomic mass (R.A.M.) given the symbol $\boldsymbol{A_r}$.

D

To work out how many atoms are present in a given mass:

$$\textbf{no. of moles} = \frac{\textbf{mass}}{\textbf{R.A.M.}\ (A_r)}$$

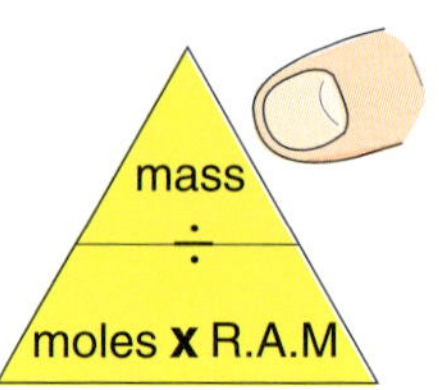

Example

How many moles of carbon atoms are there in 2.4 g of carbon (A_r of C = 12)?

number of moles = $\frac{2.4}{12}$ = **0.2 moles of carbon**

To work out the mass of atoms present:

$$\textbf{mass} = \textbf{no. of moles} \times \textbf{R.A.M.}\ (A_r)$$

To work out the number of moles of molecules / compound present:

$$\textbf{no. of moles} = \frac{\textbf{mass}}{\textbf{R.F.M.}\ (M_r)}$$

where $\boldsymbol{M_r}$ **is the relative formula mass** (R.F.M.) of a compound. To calculate $\boldsymbol{M_r}$, ***add up*** all the relative atomic masses of the elements in the compound (in the proportions shown in the chemical formula).

Example

Work out the relative formula mass (R.F.M.) of calcium carbonate, $CaCO_3$ (A_r: Ca = 40, C = 12, O = 16):

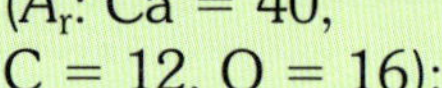

$1 \times A_r$ of Ca	=	40
$1 \times A_r$ of C	=	12
$3 \times A_r$ of O	= (3×16) =	+48
M_r of $CaCO_3$		**100**

To work out the mass of molecules / compound present:

$$\textbf{mass} = \textbf{no. of moles} \times \textbf{R.F.M.}\ (M_r)$$

Take care:

- Write down the steps in your calculation – then you can gain some marks even if your final answer is wrong!

▶ Percentage composition

D

The **percentage composition** of a compound gives us the proportion of each element present by mass, expressed in percentages.

percentage of an element in a compound

$$= \frac{\textbf{mass of that element in 1 mole of the compound}}{\textbf{relative formula mass of the compound}} \times \textbf{100}$$

We can use this to calculate the empirical formula.

Example

What is the percentage by mass of nitrogen in nitrogen dioxide, NO_2 (A_r of N = 14, O = 16)?

Mass of N in one mole of NO_2 = 14 g

Relative formula mass of NO_2 = $14 + (2 \times 16)$
= 46 g

% of N in NO_2 = $\left(\frac{14}{46}\right) \times 100 = 30.4\%$

Formulae

The simplest ratio of the numbers of moles of each element present in a compound is called its **empirical formula.**

Example

A compound of carbon and oxygen contains 3 g of carbon and 8 g of oxygen. What is its empirical formula?

Work out the ratio of moles, C : O

$$\text{Moles of carbon} = \frac{3}{12} = 0.25 \text{ moles}$$

$$\text{Moles of oxygen} = \frac{8}{16} = 0.5 \text{ moles}$$

C : O ratio is 0.25 : 0.5 = 1 : 2

Therefore the empirical formula (simplest whole number ratio) is $\mathbf{CO_2}$.

Moles of gas

Any gas, at the same temperature and pressure, contains the same number of moles of gas.

- At 20 °C and at a pressure of 1 atmosphere, 1 mole of any gas occupies 24 000 cm^3 (24 dm^3). This information is always given to you in exam questions.

  To work out the number of moles of gas in a given volume:

number of moles of gas

$$= \frac{\text{volume of gas (in cm}^3\text{)}}{24\,000 \text{ cm}^3}$$

or

number of moles of gas

$$= \frac{\text{volume of gas (in dm}^3\text{)}}{24 \text{ dm}^3}$$

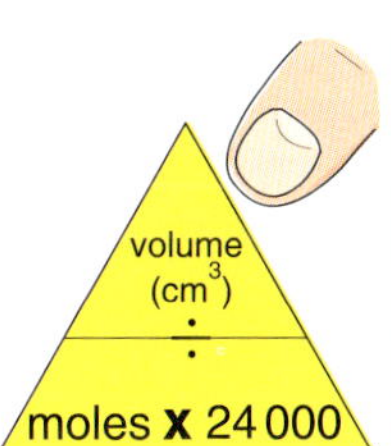

Calculations involving electrolysis

Given information about one product formed at an electrode during electrolysis, we can predict how much product is formed at the other electrode.

Example

If 4.6 g of sodium (Na) is formed at the cathode in the electrolysis of molten sodium chloride, what volume of chlorine gas is produced at the anode (A_r of Na = 23 and 1 mole of any gas at 20 °C occupies 24 000 cm^3)?

The **half equations** are:

Cathode (−): $Na^+ + e^- \longrightarrow Na$

Anode (+): $2Cl^- - 2e^- \longrightarrow Cl_2$

During the electrolysis the ***same number*** of electrons must be flowing around the circuit, so we can re-write the half-equation at the cathode as:

$$2Na^+ + 2e^- \longrightarrow 2Na$$

Therefore if we have 46 g (2 moles) of Na produced, we get 24 000 cm^3 (1 mole) of Cl_2 gas.

So 4.6 g will give **2400 cm^3 of chlorine gas.**

Calculations using balanced equations

Given a balanced equation, we can predict the masses (or volumes of any gases) involved in the chemical reaction.

Example

What volume of oxygen gas (measured at 20 °C) is given off when 8.5 g of sodium nitrate undergoes complete thermal decomposition according to the equation below (A_r of Na = 23, N = 14, O = 16 and 1 mole of any gas at 20 °C occupies 24 000 cm^3)?

$$2NaNO_3(s) \longrightarrow 2NaNO_2(s) + O_2(g)$$

The equation tells us that:

2 moles of $NaNO_3$ will give us 1 mole (24 000 cm^3) of oxygen gas.

The relative formula mass of $NaNO_3 = 23 + 14 + (3 \times 16) = 85$

Therefore 170 g (2 moles) of $NaNO_3$ will give 24 000 cm^3 of oxygen gas.

So 1 g of $NaNO_3$ will give

$$\frac{24\,000}{170} \text{ cm}^3 \text{ of oxygen gas}$$

and 8.5 g of $NaNO_3$ will give

$$\left(\frac{24\,000}{170}\right) \times 8.5 \text{ cm}^3 \text{ of oxygen gas.}$$

This gives: **1200 cm^3 of oxygen gas**

More in ***Chemistry for You,*** pages 35, 352–75.

Examination Questions – Chemical calculations

Year 11 questions

1 Iron ore contains iron oxide.

Marks

a) Calculate the relative formula mass of iron oxide, Fe_2O_3.

(Relative atomic masses: Fe = 56, O = 16)

....

....

Answer = ...

(2 marks)

b) Calculate the percentage by mass of iron in iron oxide.

....

....

Percentage of iron = ... %

(2 marks)

c) Calculate the mass of iron that could be extracted from 1000 kg of iron oxide.

Use your answer to part b) to help you with this calculation.

....

....

Mass of iron = ... kg 6

(2 marks)

2 Six thousand five hundred years ago copper ore was smelted to make copper.

a) Copper pyrites is a type of copper ore.

Calculate the relative formula mass of copper pyrites, $CuFeS_2$.

(Relative atomic masses: S = 32, Fe = 56, Cu = 64)

....

....

....

....

(1 mark)

b) Use your answer to part a) to help you calculate the percentage by mass of copper present in copper pyrites, $CuFeS_2$.

....

....

(2 marks) 3

3 The trout in a small lake were dying because the water was too acidic. Marks

Limestone, $CaCO_3$, can be used to neutralise the acid.

The equation for the reaction is:

$$CaCO_3 + H_2SO_4 \longrightarrow CaSO_4 + H_2O + CO_2$$

4900 kg of sulphuric acid in the lake needed to be neutralised.

Calculate the mass of limestone, $CaCO_3$, which reacts with this amount of sulphuric acid.

You should show **all** your working.

(Relative atomic masses: H = 1, C = 12, O = 16, S = 32, Ca = 40)

....

....

....

....

....

....

(3 marks) 3

4 A nitrogen oxide is produced by microbes in soil.

A sample of this oxide was found to contain 0.56 kg of nitrogen and 0.32 kg of oxygen.

Calculate the empirical formula of this nitrogen oxide.

You must show **all** your working to gain full marks.

(Relative atomic masses: N = 14, O = 16)

....

....

....

....

....

....

....

(4 marks) 4

Getting the Grades – Patterns of Chemical Change

Try this question, then compare your answer with the two examples opposite ▶

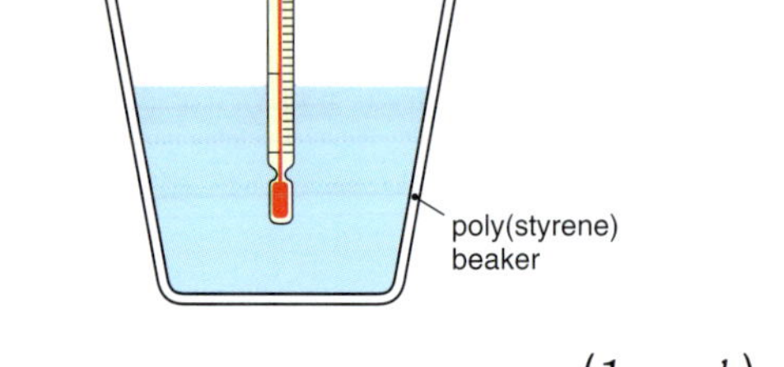

1 This question is about the energy transfers which take place when a chemical reaction happens.

The apparatus shown opposite can be used to measure the temperature changes which happen when the alkali sodium hydroxide solution is added to hydrochloric acid.

a) The reaction between these two solutions produces sodium chloride solution and water.

i Write a word equation for this reaction.

.... *(1 mark)*

ii Use the space below to sketch (not to scale) an energy level diagram to represent this reaction

(3 marks)

b) When someone burns their skin with an acid, the advice given nowadays is simply to wash the affected area with lots of water. You are advised that trying to neutralise an acid burn with an alkali will make the damage worse. Suggest why this is the case.

....

.... *(2 marks)*

c) Hydrochoric acid is formed by dissolving hydrogen chloride gas in water. Hydrogen chloride can be made by reacting hydrogen gas directly with chlorine gas. The equation for this reaction is:

$$H_2(g) + Cl_2(g) \longrightarrow 2HCl(g)$$

Bond energies can be used to estimate the energy change for a reaction like this.

The relevant bond energies are:

Bond	**Energy (kJ /mol)**
H—H	436
Cl—Cl	242
H—Cl	431

Some of the necessary calculations have been performed below:
Use the information above to complete all stages in the calculations below:

i

Bonds broken		**Bonds formed**	
number × type	bond energies / kJ/mol	number × type	bond energies
1 × H—H	*1 × 436 = 436*		
1 × Cl—Cl			
Total energy	*678*		

(4 marks)

ii Estimate the energy change for this reaction.

.... *(2 marks)*

[*Total 12 marks*]

GRADE 'A' ANSWER

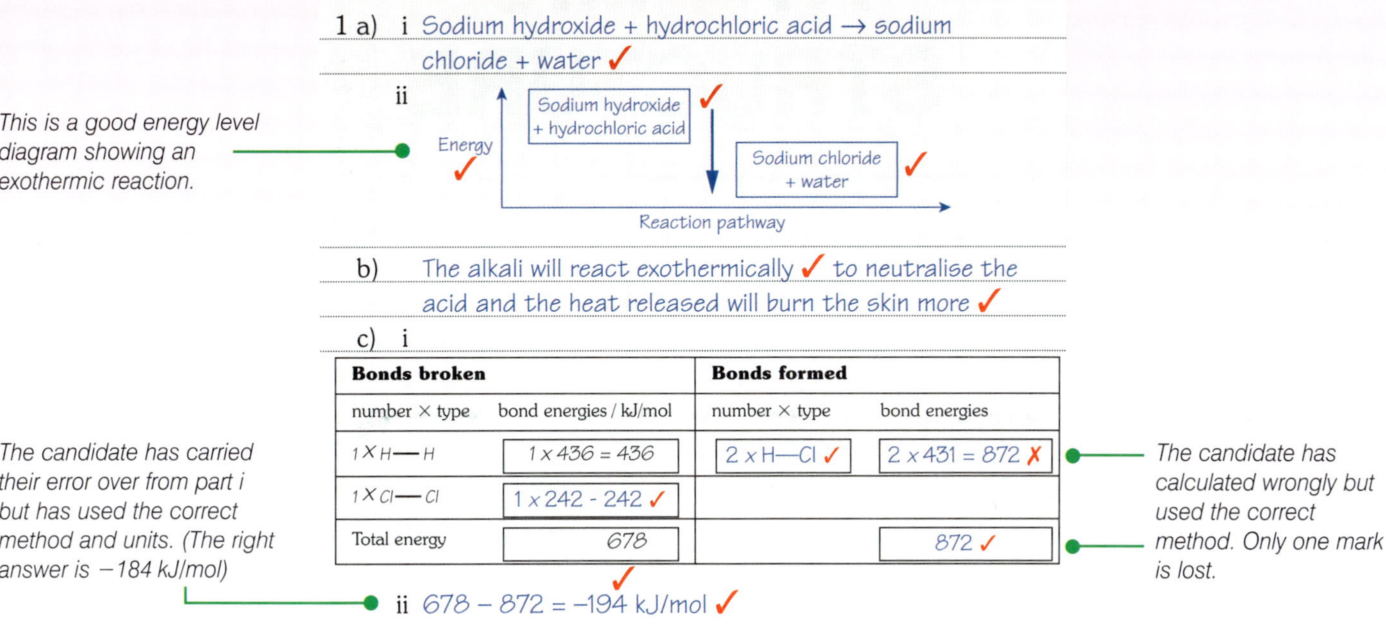
1 a) i Sodium hydroxide + hydrochloric acid → sodium chloride + water ✓

ii

This is a good energy level diagram showing an exothermic reaction.

b) The alkali will react exothermically ✓ to neutralise the acid and the heat released will burn the skin more ✓

c) i

Bonds broken		**Bonds formed**	
number × type	bond energies / kJ/mol	number × type	bond energies
1 × H—H	1 x 436 = 436	2 x H—Cl ✓	2 x 431 = 872 ✗
1 × Cl—Cl	1 x 242 - 242 ✓		
Total energy	678		872 ✓

ii 678 – 872 = –194 kJ/mol ✓ ✓

The candidate has carried their error over from part i but has used the correct method and units. (The right answer is −184 kJ/mol)

The candidate has calculated wrongly but used the correct method. Only one mark is lost.

11 marks = Grade A answer

Improve your Grades A up to A*

This answer is very good, with only a small arithmetic error losing one mark. In this question a table was provided to organise your data. It is worth getting used to organising your calculations in this way as in all calculations workings can pick up marks.

GRADE 'C' ANSWER

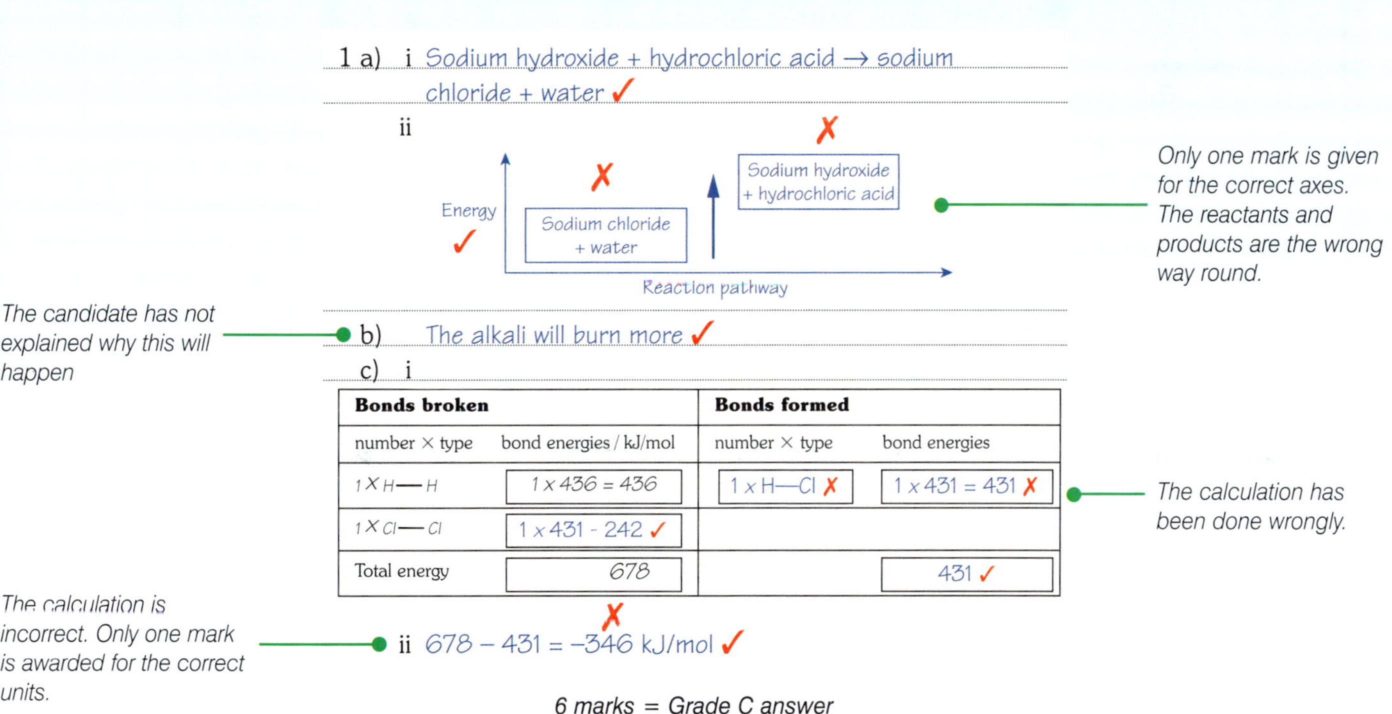
1 a) i Sodium hydroxide + hydrochloric acid → sodium chloride + water ✓

ii

Only one mark is given for the correct axes. The reactants and products are the wrong way round.

The candidate has not explained why this will happen

b) The alkali will burn more ✓

c) i

Bonds broken		**Bonds formed**	
number × type	bond energies / kJ/mol	number × type	bond energies
1 × H—H	1 x 436 = 436	1 x H—Cl ✗	1 x 431 = 431 ✗
1 × Cl—Cl	1 x 431 - 242 ✓		
Total energy	678		431 ✓

The calculation has been done wrongly.

ii 678 – 431 = –346 kJ/mol ✗ ✓

The calculation is incorrect. Only one mark is awarded for the correct units.

6 marks = Grade C answer

Improve your Grades C up to B

The mistake made with the energy level diagram is the result of confusing temperature and energy. Think of an exothermic reaction as a beaker of reacting liquid becoming hot. Eventually it will cool down to a temperature equal to its surroundings. As a result of this, it will have lost energy. Thus the energy level of the product will be lower than that of the reactant.

14

ATOMIC STRUCTURE

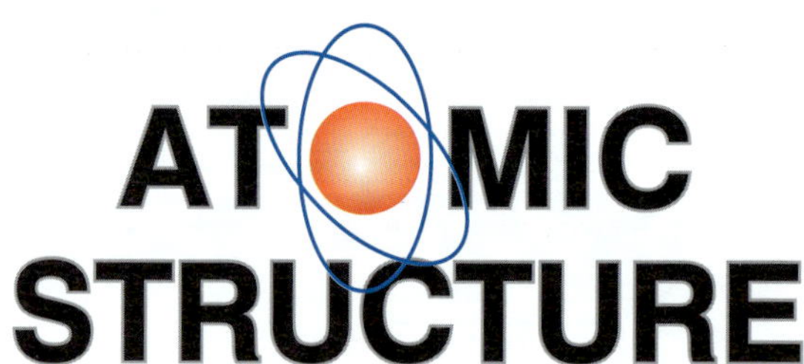

ThinkAbout:

1 Name the three types of sub-atomic particle found inside atoms.
2 Which of the sub-atomic particles carries a negative charge?
3 Which of the sub-atomic particles is neutral?
4 An atom has a mass number of 7 and an atomic number of 3. How many  of each type of sub-atomic particle does it contain?
5 What is the difference between the atoms of isotopes of an element?

Inside atoms

Some Ancient Greeks thought that all substances are made up from tiny particles called atoms. It was an English scientist called John Dalton, about 200 years ago, who revived this theory.

Dalton called substances that he thought contained only one type of atom 'elements'.

We have now discovered about 100 different elements.

Inside atoms we find **protons, neutrons and electrons**.

The protons and neutrons are in the centre of the atom called the **nucleus**. This is where the mass is concentrated.

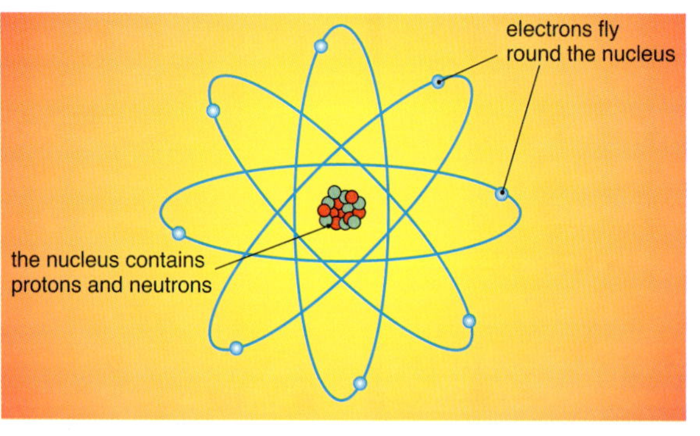

Here are the properties of these sub-atomic particles:

Particle	Charge	Mass (in atomic mass units)
proton	1+	1
neutron	0	1
electron	1−	0 (almost)

Electronic structures

The electrons whizz around the nucleus in **shells** (or **energy levels**).

The first shell holds up to **2** electrons.
The second shell can hold up to **8** electrons.
The third shell holds **8** electrons.

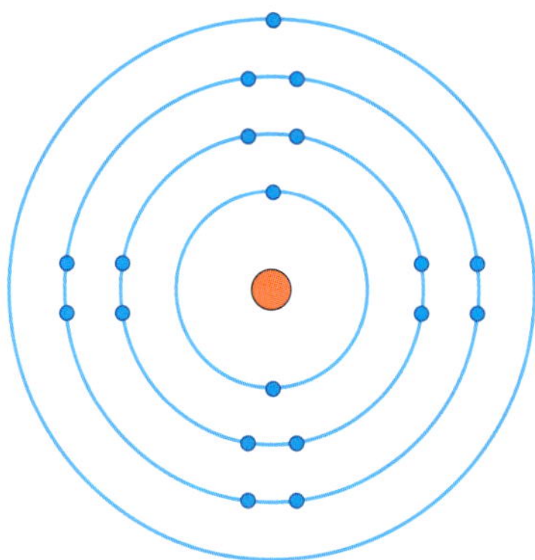

We can show an atom's **electronic structure** quickly using numbers. This tells us the arrangement of electrons around the nucleus, starting with the electrons in the innermost shell.

So, the electronic structure of a potassium atom (shown above) is 2, 8, 8, 1.

The largest atom you need to work out the electronic structure for is calcium.

Its atomic number is 20. Therefore its electronic structure is 2, 8, 8, 2.

Answers: 1 protons, neutrons, electrons 2 electrons 3 neutrons 4 It has 3 protons, 3 electrons and 4 neutrons. 5 They contain different numbers of neutrons.

Atomic number

D

> The **atomic number** tells us how many protons there are in an atom.

This also equals the number of electrons. That's because atoms themselves are neutral, therefore they must have the same number of protons (+) as electrons (−).

Mass number

> The **mass number** tells us the number of protons plus neutrons.

We can show these like this:

mass number ⟶ 14
atomic number ⟶ 7

$^{14}_{7}\mathrm{N}$

Isotopes

D

The atoms of any particular element always contain the same number of electrons. However, their number of neutrons can differ.

Isotopes of an element contain different numbers of neutrons. Look at the examples below:

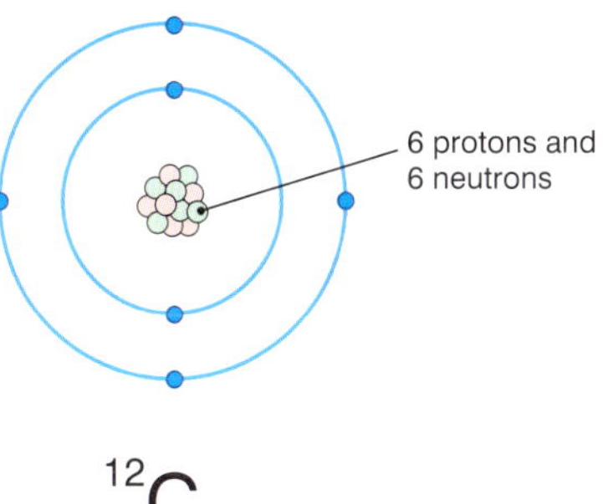

6 protons and 8 neutrons

$^{12}_{6}\mathrm{C}$ $^{14}_{6}\mathrm{C}$

As you can see from this example:

> **Isotopes** of an element have the same atomic number but different mass numbers.

Isotopes are a bit like Easter eggs which have the same chocolate shell, but different numbers of sweets inside !

Take care:

The isotopes of an element undergo all the same reactions. That's because chemical properties rely on electronic structures. In isotopes of an element the arrangement of electrons is identical (see above).

More in ***Chemistry for You***, pages 28–33.

Examination Questions – Atomic structure

Year 11 questions

Marks

1 a) The diagram represents an atom. Choose words from the list to label the particles.

electron **ion** **neutron** **proton**

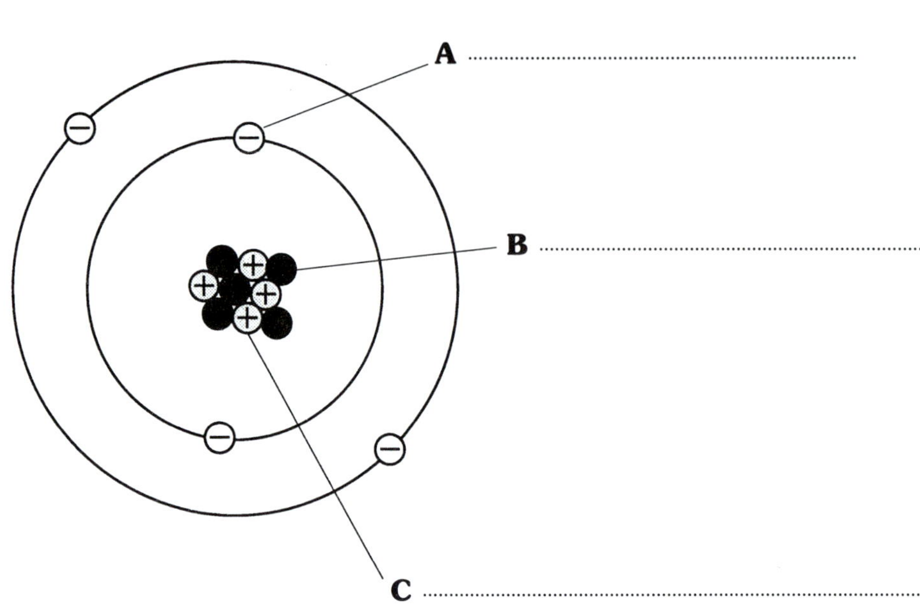

(3 marks)

b) An atom of magnesium can be represented by the symbol ${}^{24}_{12}Mg$.

Draw a **ring** around the letter, **A** to **D**, in the table which correctly describes the atomic structure of magnesium.

	PROTONS	ELECTRONS	NEUTRONS
A	6	6	6
B	12	12	12
C	24	12	12
D	36	12	12

(1 mark)

c) i The atomic number of aluminium is 13.
How many electrons are found in the outer shell (highest energy level) of an aluminium atom?

....

(1 mark)

ii What will be the charge on an aluminium ion?

....

(1 mark)

iii An aluminium atom contains 14 neutrons. What is its mass number?

....

(1 mark) 7

2 Use the information about a phosphorus atom to complete the table. Marks

$^{31}_{15}\mathbf{P}$

	the number of protons is	a) ....
In one atom of phosphorus ...	the number of neutrons is	b) ....
	the number of electrons is	c) ....

3 a) A diagram of the nucleus of an atom is shown below.

i Draw a diagram to show the electronic arrangement of this atom.

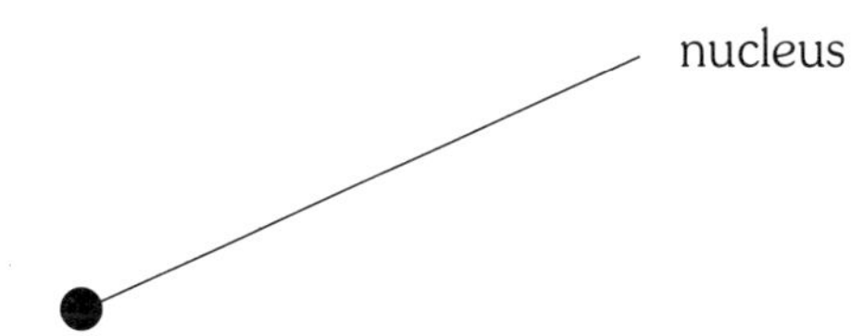

(1 mark)

ii What is the mass number of this atom?

....

(1 mark)

iii Use the table on page 118 to give the chemical symbol for this element.

....

(1 mark)

b) Name the particle in an atom that carries no overall charge.

....

(1 mark) 4

15 Bonding

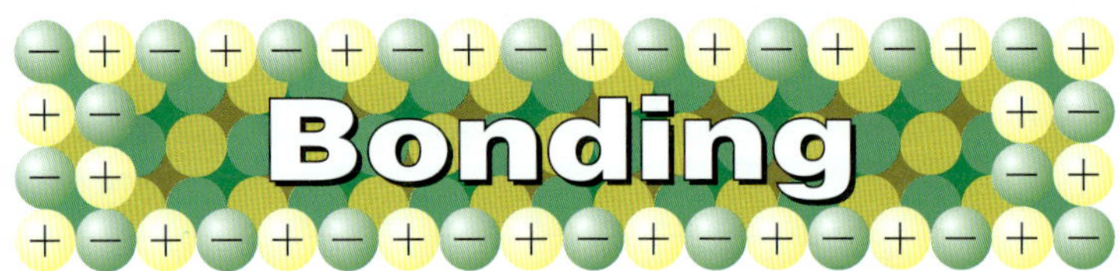

ThinkAbout:

1. Describe the movement of the particles in a solid.
2. What happens to the particles in a solid as they are warmed up?
3. What is the difference between an atom and an ion?
4. Explain what a chemical compound is.
5. Write the formula of the ions found in sodium chloride.
6. How many electrons are shared in a single covalent bond?

Ionic bonding

D

Metals bond to non-metals in **ionic compounds**. (A compound is a substance in which atoms of two, or more, elements are chemically combined.)

The metal atom gives one, or more, electrons to the non-metal atom.

This happens as the elements react together.

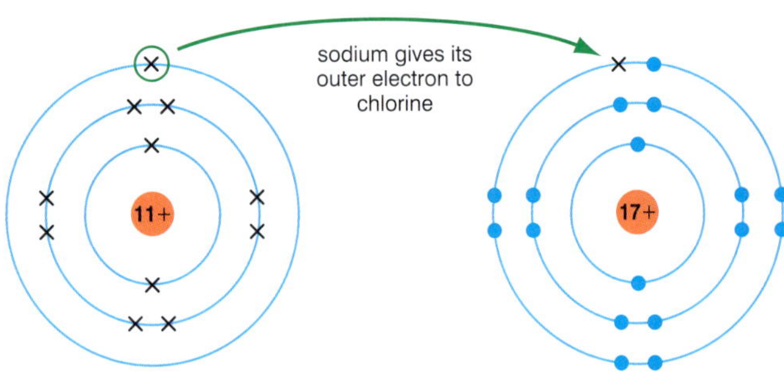

The charged particles formed are called **ions**.

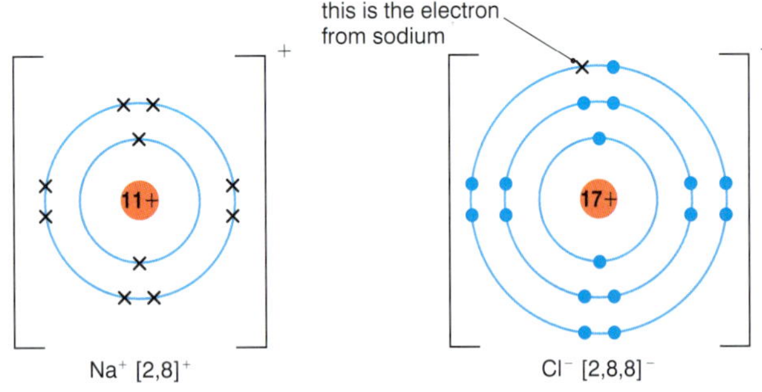

The attractions between oppositely charged ions are called **ionic bonds**.

- Metal atoms form positive ions (for example, Na^+, Mg^{2+}, Al^{3+}).
- Atoms of non-metals form negative ions (for example, Cl^-, O^{2-}).

Structure and properties of ionic compounds

D

The ions form regular structures called **giant ionic lattices**.

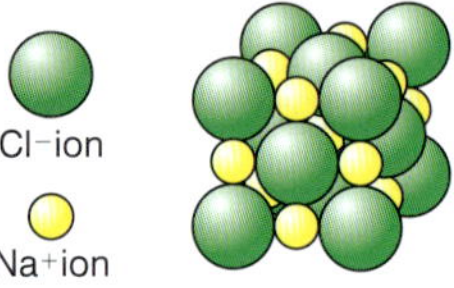

- There are strong forces of attraction between millions of oppositely charged ions.
- So ionic compounds have high melting points.

D H

Ionic compounds don't conduct electricity when they are solid. However, they do if you melt them or dissolve them in water. The ions are then free to move around and carry the charge through the liquid.

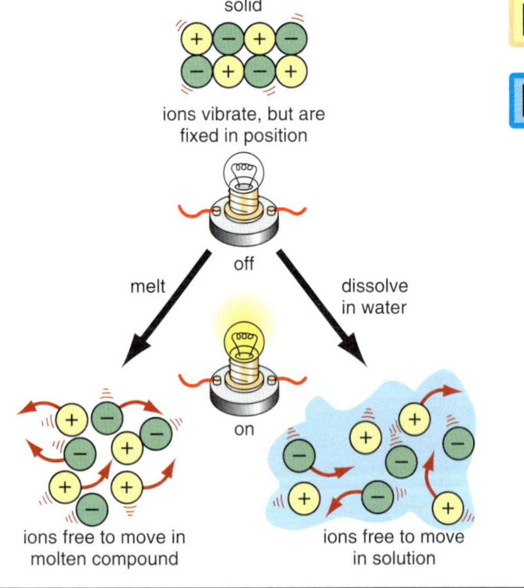

Answers: **1** They vibrate. **2** They vibrate more vigorously (quickly). **3** Atoms are neutral, whereas ions are charged. **4** A substance made of two or more types of atom bonded together. **5** Na^+ and Cl^- **6** 2 electrons

Covalent bonding

Atoms of non-metals can bond to each other by **sharing pairs of electrons**.

This is **covalent bonding**.

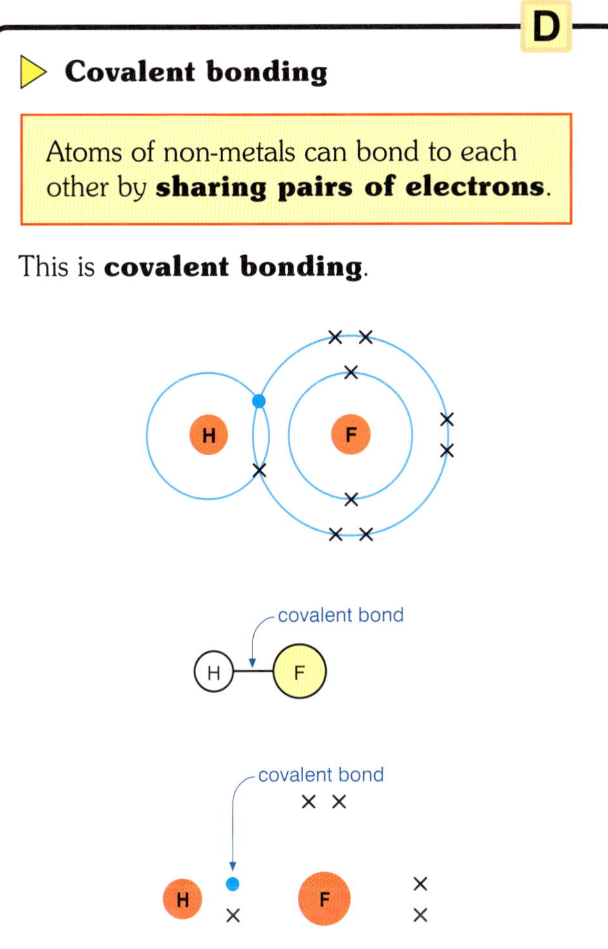

Properties of covalent substances

Many covalently bonded substances are made up of small individual molecules (for example, water).
These have low melting points and boiling points because the forces ***between*** molecules are relatively weak.

Other substances with covalent bonds have **giant covalent structures**.

These have very high melting points (for example, diamond and graphite).

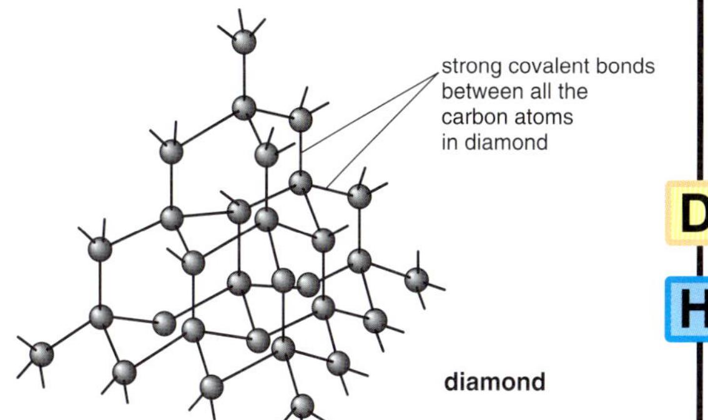

D
H

Graphite is the only non-metallic element that is a good conductor of electricity.

Look at the diagram below:

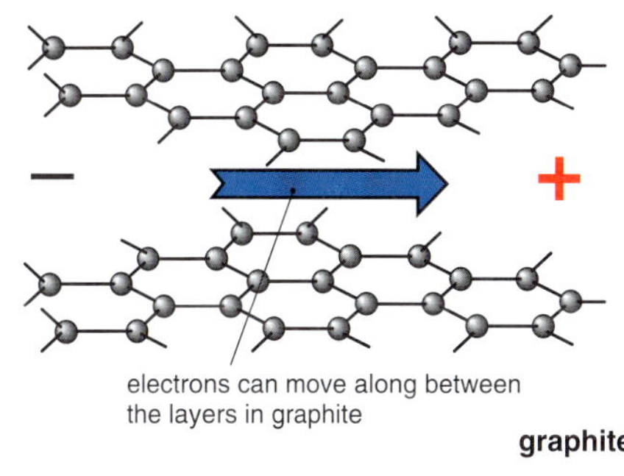

Take care:
Atoms that lose electrons form positive ions – they have more protons than electrons in their ions!

D H

Metallic bonding

The atoms (or positive ions) in a metal are held to each other by a 'sea' of free electrons. These electrons:

- hold the atoms (or ions) together in giant structures,
- can drift though the metal when it conducts,
- let the atoms (or ions) slip over each other when hit or stretched.

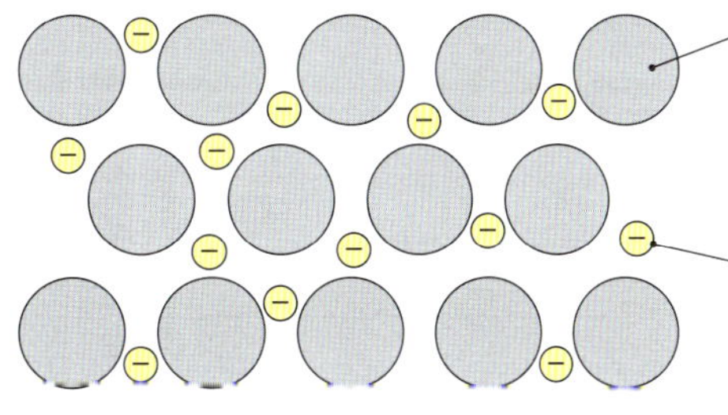

More in ***Chemistry for You***, pages 262–86.

Examination Questions – Bonding

Year 11 questions

1 The diagram shows a model of part of the giant lattice of a metal. Marks

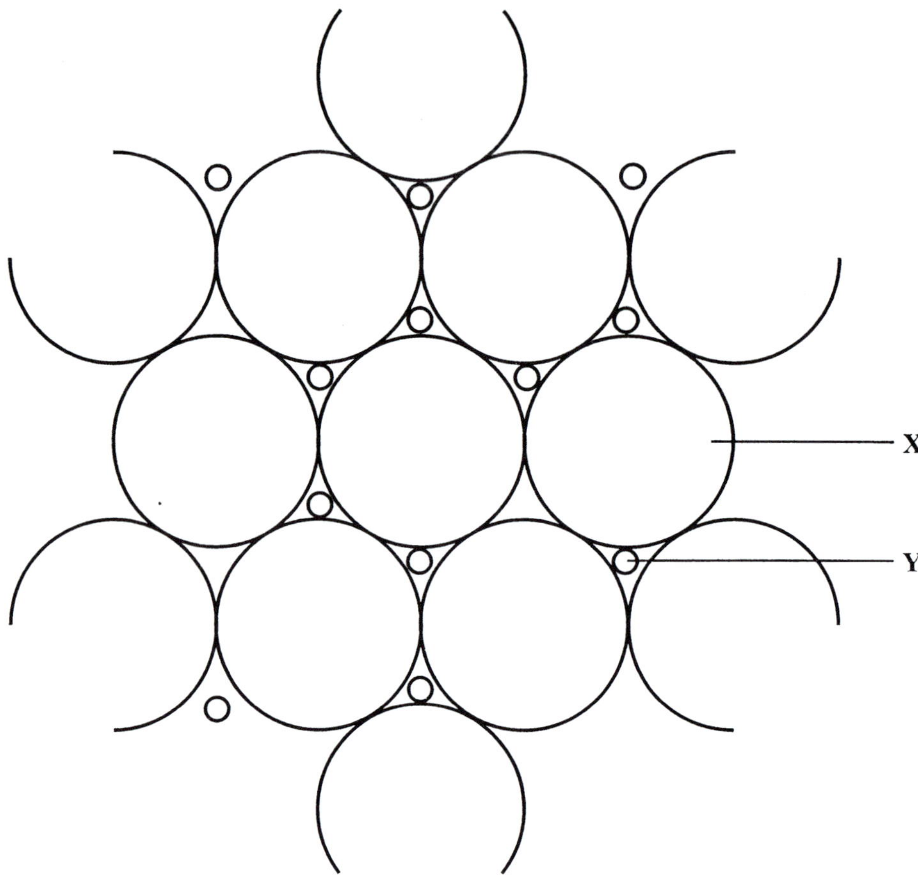

a) Name particles **X** and **Y**.

X ....

Y .... *(2 marks)*

b) Explain in terms of the giant structure above, why it is possible to bend a piece of metal.

....

....

....

....

(2 marks)

c) Why can metals conduct electricity?

....

....

....

(2 marks) 6

2 Magnesium burns in oxygen to form magnesium oxide. Marks

a) Balance the equation for the reaction between magnesium and oxygen.

$$\text{.......}Mg + O_2 \longrightarrow \text{.......}MgO$$

(1 mark)

b) Use pages 117 and 118 to help you answer these questions.

i The electronic structure of a magnesium atom can be represented as shown below. Draw a similar diagram for an oxygen atom.

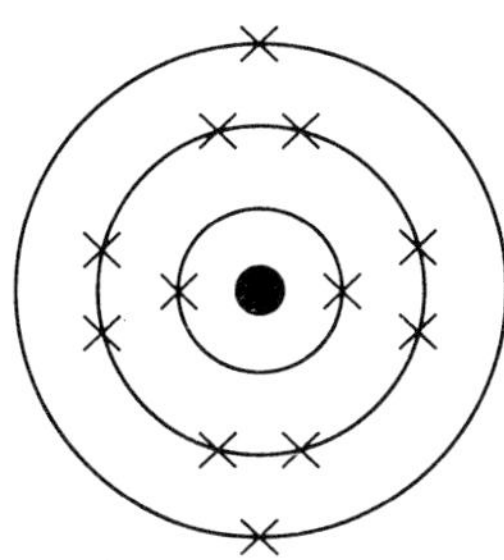

magnesium atom　　　　oxygen atom　　　　*(1 mark)*

ii The electronic structure of an oxide ion can be represented as shown below. Draw a similar diagram to show the electronic structure of a magnesium ion.

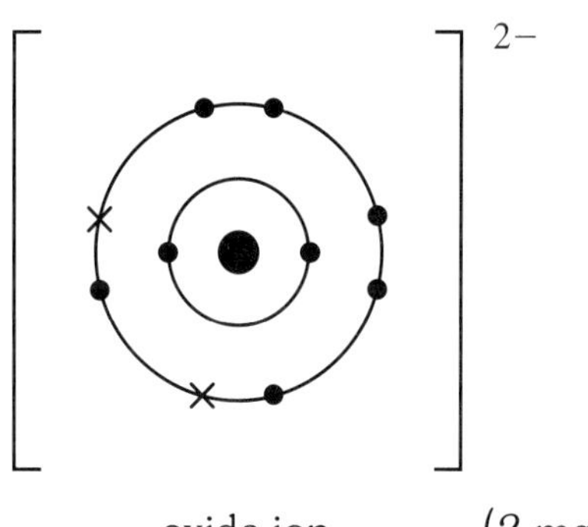

magnesium ion　　　　oxide ion　　　　*(2 marks)*

c) Magnesium oxide is used in making linings for furnaces. Explain why ionic substances, such as magnesium oxide, have high melting points.

....

....

....

....

(2 marks)

d) The elements in Group 2, like the elements in Group 1, become more reactive lower down the Group. Explain why.

....

....

....

....

(3 marks) 9

16

The Periodic Table

ThinkAbout:

1 Are there more metallic or non-metallic elements in the Periodic Table?

2 What nationality was the chemist who developed the Periodic Table?

3 In which part of the Periodic Table do you find the group of metals that are most reactive?

4 Which elements are represented by:
a) Ca b) Mg c) S d) Si

History of the Periodic Table

In the nineteenth century chemists were busy trying to find the fundamental patterns that linked the chemical elements. An English scientist called John Newlands had a little success when he tried listing the elements in order of their atomic mass. He noticed that every eighth element was similar. Unfortunately, the pattern broke down after the first 15 of the elements known at that time.

However, he was on the right lines; in 1869 a Russian chemist, called Dmitri Mendeleev, solved the problem. He left gaps in his table of elements so that similar elements always lined up in columns. He argued that the gaps would be filled when new elements were discovered.

He even predicted the properties of missing elements from the patterns he could see in his Periodic Table. Other scientists accepted his theory when his predictions proved remarkably accurate.

Some strange things remained unanswered about the Periodic Table. Mendeleev had changed the order of a few elements so that they could line up in their groups, but why?

We now know that the Periodic Table is related to the structure of the atoms of each element. They should be arranged according to their atomic numbers, not their atomic masses (see page 118).

Atomic number	Element	Electronic structure	Atomic number	Element	Electronic structure
1	H	1	11	Na	2,8,1
2	He	2	12	Mg	2,8,2
3	Li	2,1	13	Al	2,8,3
4	Be	2,2	14	Si	2,8,4
5	B	2,3	15	P	2,8,5
6	C	2,4	16	S	2,8,6
7	N	2,5	17	Cl	2,8,7
8	O	2,6	18	Ar	2,8,8
9	F	2,7	19	K	2,8,8,1
10	Ne	2,8	20	Ca	2,8,8,2

Electrons and the Periodic Table

The chemical properties of elements are determined by the electronic structures of their atoms.

The number of electrons in the **outer shell** (or highest energy level) is important.

Group 1 metals react by losing their single outer electron. They get more reactive going down the group. That's because it gets easier to lose that outer electron the further away it gets from the attractive force of the nucleus.

H

The opposite is true of the non-metals in Group 7. Their elements react with metals by gaining an extra electron into their outer shell. They get less reactive going down the group, as the larger atoms find it more difficult to attract an electron into their outer shell. That is because the incoming electron is further away from the attractive force of the positively charged nucleus.

The Group 0 elements are so unreactive because their outer shells are complete already. They have no tendency to lose or to gain electrons.

Answers: **1** metallic **2** Russian **3** Group 1 (far left) **4** a) calcium b) magnesium c) sulphur d) silicon

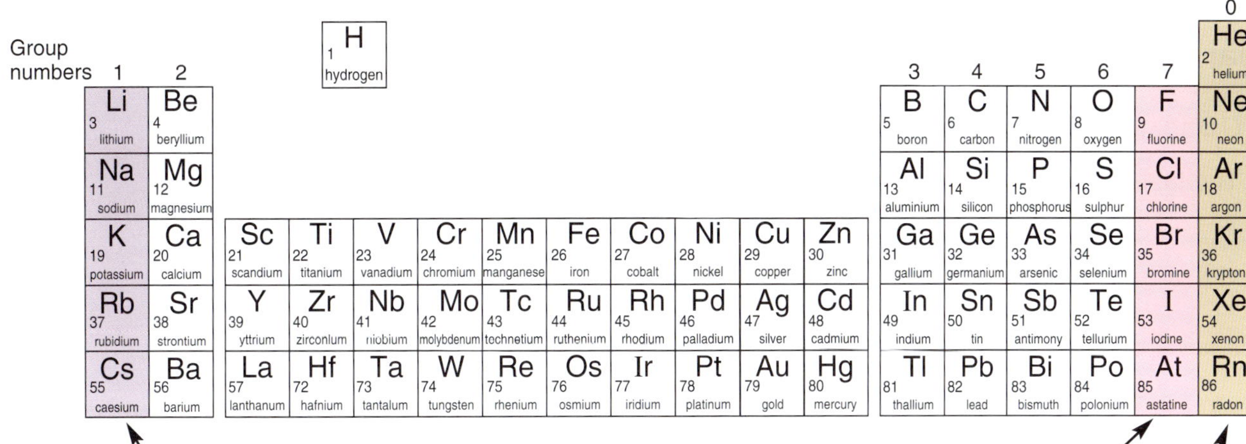

▷ **Group 1** elements are the metals called the **alkali metals**.

- They react with non-metals to produce ionic compounds, forming ions with a 1+ charge.
- When dropped on to water, they fizz around the surface giving off hydrogen gas and forming an alkaline solution of the metal hydroxide.

▷ **Group 7** elements are the non-metals called the **halogens**.

- They react with metals to produce ionic salts, forming ions with a 1− charge.
- They react with other non-metals to form molecules, in which the atoms are joined by covalent bonds.
- They all have coloured vapours and exist as diatomic molecules, for example, F_2.
- They become less reactive going down the group.
- Their melting points and boiling points increase going down the group.

▷ **Group 0** are the very un-reactive **noble gases**.

- They exist as single atoms (monatomic gases).
- Helium is less dense than air and is used in airships and balloons.
- The gases are also used inside electric discharge tubes where they glow brightly. For example, neon glows red.
- Their boiling points and density increase going down the group.

Groups are families of elements. The members of the family are similar but not exactly the same.

More in ***Chemistry for You***, pages 42–72.

Examination Questions – The Periodic Table

Year 11 questions

Marks

1 Use the periodic table on the Data Sheet (see page 118) to answer these questions.

The table below gives the electronic structures of four elements, **W**, **X**, **Y** and **Z**.

Element	Electronic structure
W	2,5
X	2,7
Y	2,8,8
Z	2,8,8,1

a) Which element **W**, **X**, **Y** or **Z**:

i Is a Group 0 gas? ....

ii Is nitrogen? ....

iii Is a Group 7 gas? ....

iv Reacts violently with water? .... *(3 marks)*

b) Which **two** Groups of the periodic table do **not** contain any metals?

....

(2 marks) 5

2 The picture shows part of a "Chemical Elements" tie, manufactured by "Scienceshirts".

Look at the picture of the tie and then compare it with the Periodic Table on page 118.

a) What do the numbers on the tie represent?

.... *(1 mark)*

b) In the modern Periodic Table the elements are arranged in Groups.

Why is this arrangement more useful than the arrangement in Columns on the tie?

....

....

....

.... *(1 mark)*

c) Choose from **Column F** of the tie the symbol of an element which:

i is in Group 2 of the modern Periodic Table; ....

ii is a noble gas; ....

iii is an alkali metal; ....

iv has atoms with an electron arrangement, 2,8,5; ....

v is not included in the Periodic Table on page 118. ....

(5 marks) 7

Column	A	B	C	D	E	F	G
	B	1 H	2 He	3 Li	4 Be	5 B	1 H
	le	6 C	7 N	8 O	9 F	10 Ne	6 C
	P	11 Na	12 Mg	13 Al	14 Si	15 P	11 Na
	Ca	16 S	17 Cl	18 Ar	19 K	20 Ca	16 S
	Mn	21 Sc	22 Ti	23 V	24 Cr	25 Mn	21 Sc
	Zn	26 Fe	27 Co	28 Ni	29 Cu	30 Zn	26 Fe
	Br	31 Ga	32 Ge	33 As	34 Se	35 Br	31 Ga
	40 Zr	36 Kr	37 Rb	38 Sr	39 Y	40 Zr	36 Kr
	45 Rh	41 Nb	42 Mo	43 Tc	44 Ru	45 Rh	41 Nb
	50 Sn	46 Pd	47 Ag	48 Cd	49 In	50 Sn	46 Pd
	55 Cs	51 Sb	52 Te	53 I	54 Xe	55 Cs	51 Sb
	60 Nd	56 Ba	57 La	58 Ce	59 Pr	60 Nd	56 Ba
	65 Tb	61 Pm	62 Sm	63 Eu	64 Gd	65 Tb	61 Pm
	70 Yb	66 Dy	67 Ho	68 Er	69 Tm	70 Yb	66 Dy
	75 Re	71 Lu	72 Hf	73 Ta	74 W	75 Re	71 Lu
	80 Hg	76 Os	77 Ir	78 Pt	79 Au	80 Hg	76 Os
	85 At	81 Tl	82 Pb	83 Bi	84 Po	85 At	81 Tl
	90 Th	86 Rn	87 Fr	88 Ra	89 Ac	90 Th	86 Rn
	95 Am	91 Pa	92 U	93 Np	94 Pu	95 Am	91 Pa
	100 Fm	96 Cm	97 Bk	98 Cf	99 Es	100 Fm	96 Cm
	105 Ha	101 Md	102 No	103 Lr	104 Rf	105 Ha	101 Md
		1 H	2 He	3 Li	4 Be	5 B	
			7 N	8 O	9 F		
				13 Al			

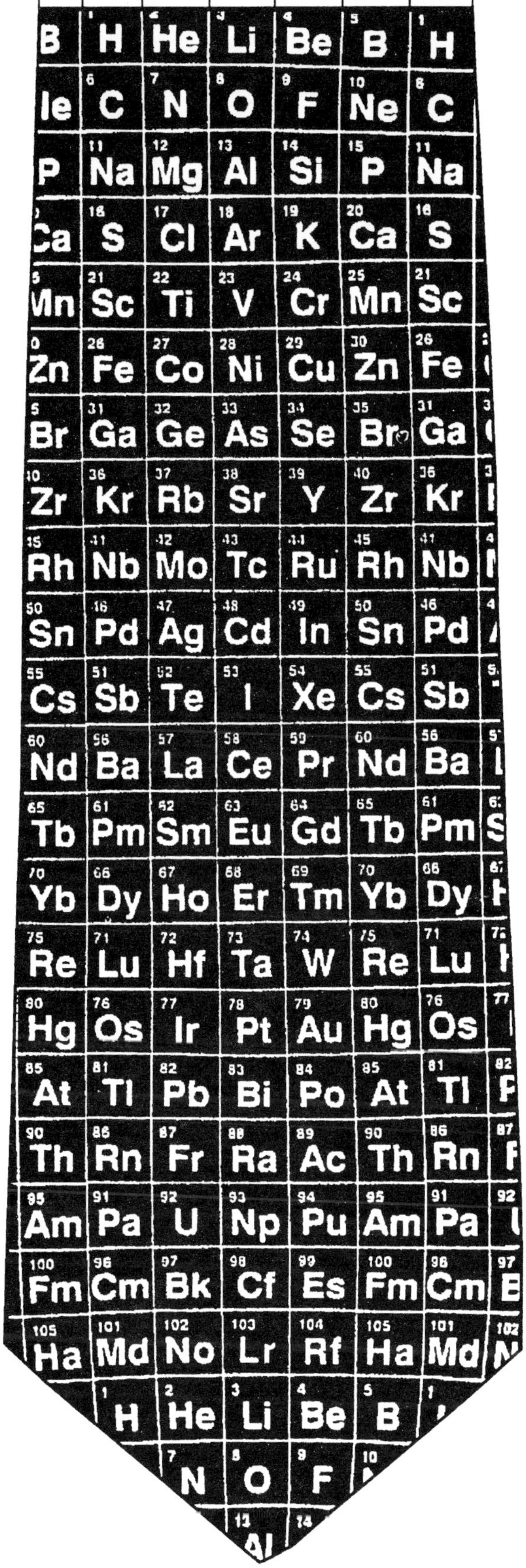

17

ThinkAbout:

1 What is the chemical formula of sodium chloride?

2 What type of bonding do we find in sodium chloride?

3 How do the elements, sodium and chlorine, differ from the compound, sodium chloride?

Sodium chloride – common salt

D

We find sodium chloride naturally in the sea and underground as rock salt. It can be pumped up from underground as **brine** (salt solution).

The brine is electrolysed in industry to form **hydrogen, chlorine** and **sodium hydroxide** solution.

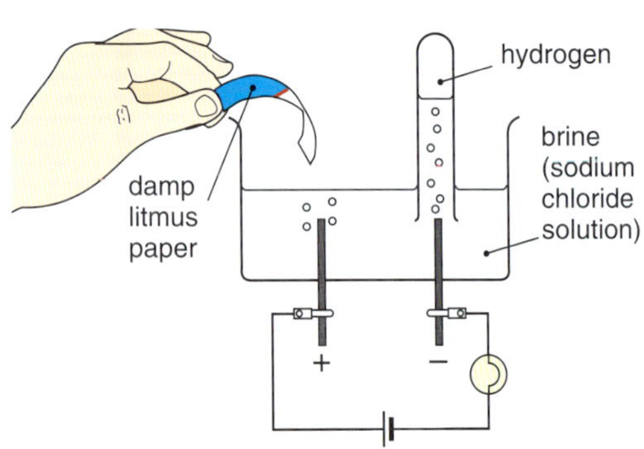

- Hydrogen is given off from the negative electrode.
  (Hydrogen makes a 'pop' – a squeaky explosion – with a lighted splint).
- Chlorine gas is given off from the positive electrode.
  (Chlorine bleaches damp litmus paper).
- The solution around the negative electrode turns alkaline (as acidic $H^+(aq)$ ions are removed). This eventually turns the brine into sodium hydroxide solution.

More salts – silver halides

D

Silver halides are used in photographic film and paper.

They are broken down and reduced to silver by light, X-rays or radioactivity.

e.g.

$$\text{silver bromide} \xrightarrow{\text{light}} \text{silver} + \text{bromine}$$

$$2AgBr \longrightarrow 2Ag + Br_2$$

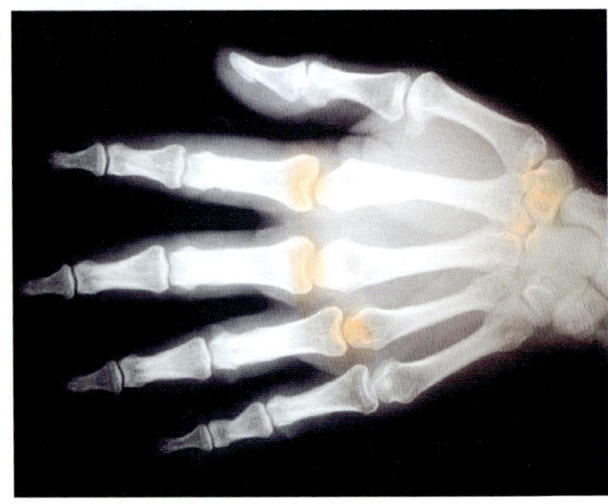

Answers: **1** NaCl **2** ionic bonding **3** Sodium is a reactive metal, stored under oil. Chlorine is a green/yellow toxic gas. Sodium chloride is the white crystalline compound known as common salt.

Useful products from sodium chloride

D

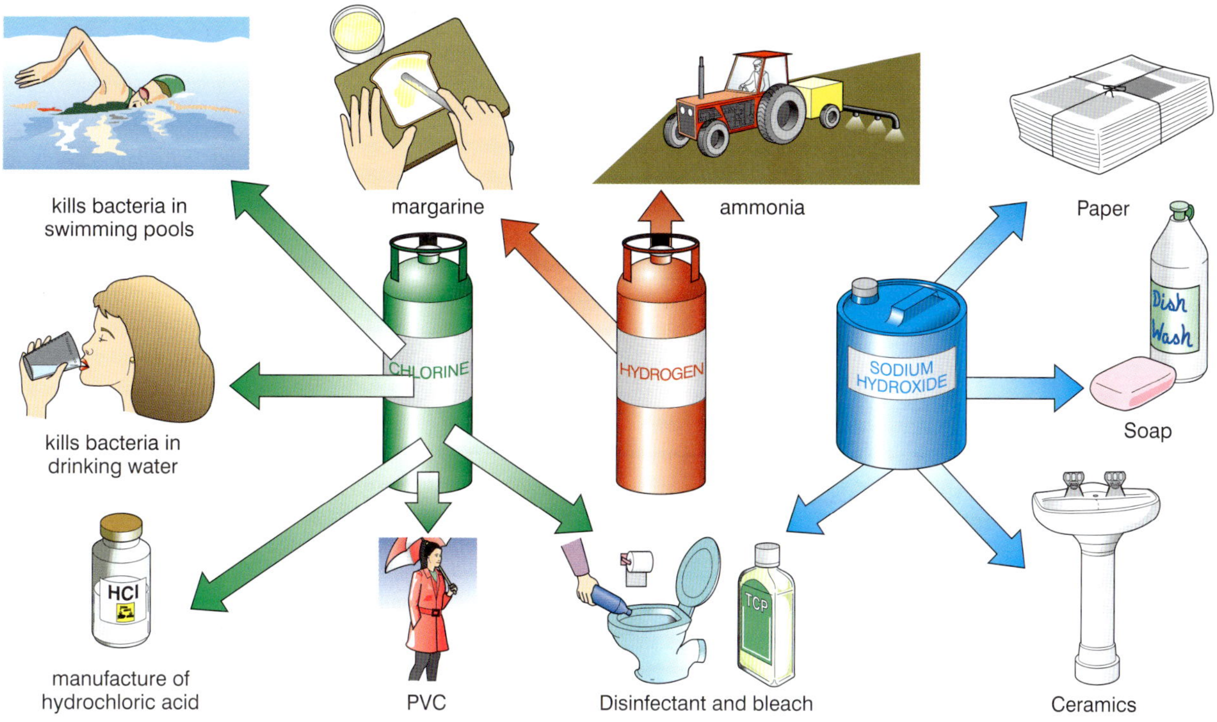
kills bacteria in swimming pools
margarine
ammonia
Paper
kills bacteria in drinking water
CHLORINE
HYDROGEN
SODIUM HYDROXIDE
Dish Wash
Soap
HCl
manufacture of hydrochloric acid
PVC
TCP
Disinfectant and bleach
Ceramics

More acids – the hydrogen halides

- Hydrogen halides, e.g. HCl, HBr and HI, are gases.
- They dissolve in water to form **acidic solutions**.

D

H Cl
hydrogen chloride gas
dissolve in water
funnel
H + Cl −
hydrochloric acid

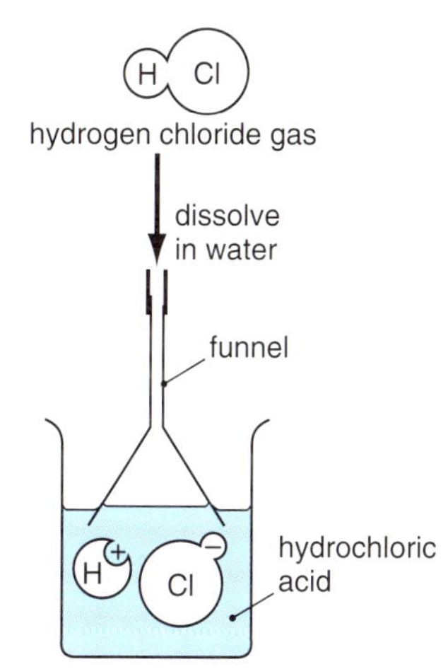

Displacement reactions

A more reactive halogen can displace a less reactive halogen from a solution of its halide salt.

E.g.

bromine + sodium iodide ⟶ sodium bromide + iodine

$$Br_2(aq) + 2\,NaI(aq) \longrightarrow 2\,NaBr(aq) + I_2(aq)$$

Bromine displaces iodide ions from solution. This shows that bromine is more reactive than iodine.

Look at another example:

chlorine solution
potassium bromide turns yellow as bromine is displaced

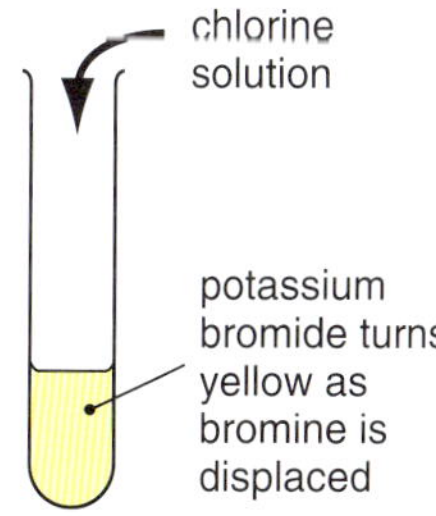

More in ***Chemistry for You***, pages 118–26, 142– 58, 268

Examination Questions – Metal halides

Year 11 questions

1 The diagram shows the electrolysis of sodium chloride solution.

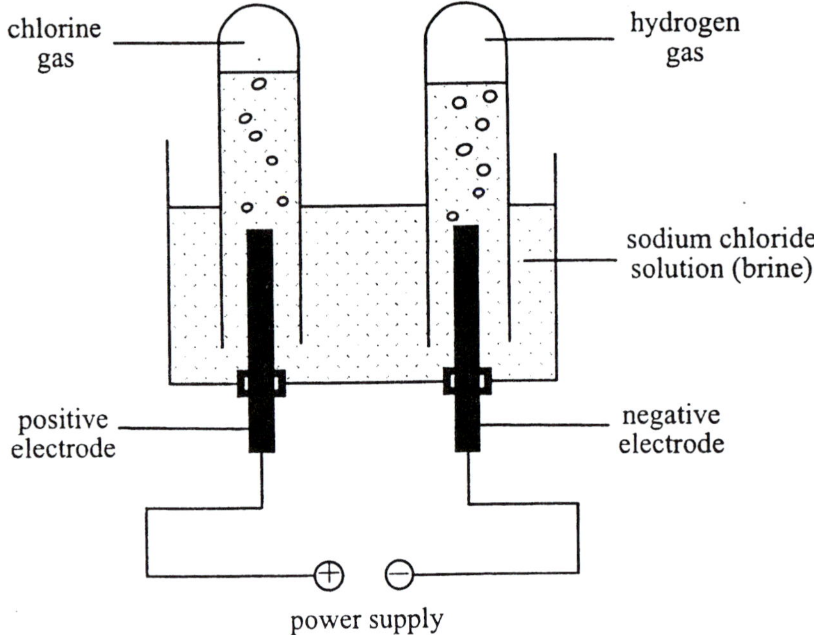

Marks

a) i You can test for chlorine gas using moist litmus paper.

What happens to the litmus paper?

....

(1 mark)

ii Describe how you can test the gas in the other tube to show that it is hydrogen.

(You should also give the result of the test).

....

....

(1 mark)

b) This symbol equation shows one reaction of chlorine.

$$Cl_2 + 2NaBr \longrightarrow 2NaCl + Br_2$$

i Write a word equation for this reaction.

.... + ... $\longrightarrow$ .... + ...

(1 mark)

ii What does this reaction tell you about the reactivity of chlorine and bromine? Explain your answer.

....

....

....

(2 marks) 5

2 a) Sodium chloride is an ionic compound. Marks

This is a diagram of a sodium ion. Complete this diagram of a chloride ion.

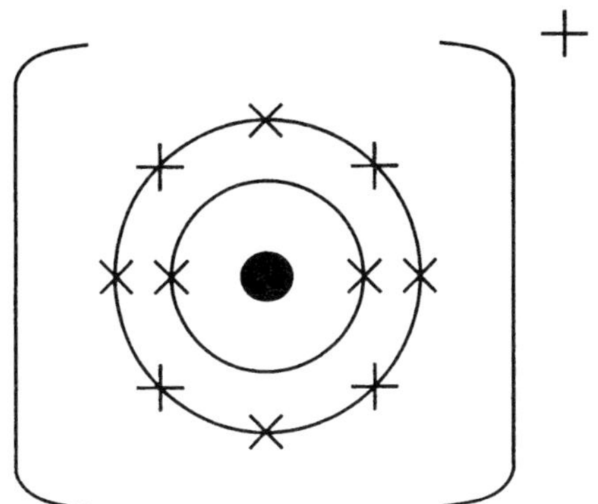

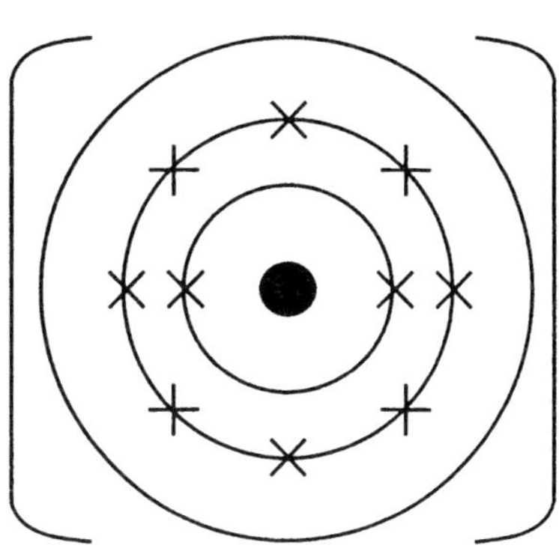

(*2 marks*)

b) The electrolysis of sodium chloride produces chlorine.

Chlorine is used to produce bleach (HOCl).

This equation represents the reaction.

$$Cl_2(g) + H_2O(l) \longrightarrow HCl(aq) + HOCl(aq)$$

Give the meaning of the state symbols (l) and (aq).

(l) ....

(aq) ....

(*2 marks*)

c) The equation below represents the reaction between chlorine and potassium bromide.

$$Cl_2(aq) + KBr(aq) \longrightarrow KCl(aq) + Br_2(aq)$$

i Balance this equation. (*1 mark*)

ii Why does chlorine displace bromine from potassium bromide solution?

....

....

(*1 mark*) 6

3 A precipitate of silver chloride will darken if we leave it in sunlight.

a) Which product of the reaction causes the dark colour?

....

(*1 mark*)

b) Write a word equation for the reaction.

....

(*2 marks*)

c) What is this type of reaction called?

....

(*1 mark*) 4

18 Representing reactions

ThinkAbout:

1 Hydrogen chloride gas is formed when hydrogen burns in chlorine gas. Write a word equation for this reaction.

2 Write a balanced equation, including state symbols, for the reaction described in question 1. (Chemical formulae needed: hydrogen = H_2, chlorine = Cl_2, hydrogen chloride = HCl)

Conservation of mass

We can classify changes as physical changes or chemical changes:

- **Physical changes** do not produce any new substances, and are often easy to reverse. Changes of state, such as melting or boiling, are examples of physical changes.
- However, in **chemical changes** (or reactions) new substances are made. There are energy changes that accompany chemical changes. Burning carbon is an example of a chemical change.

We can represent these chemical reactions by **word equations**:

reactants ⟶ products

For example:

carbon + oxygen ⟶ carbon dioxide

The law of **conservation of mass** states that:

the total mass of the reactants equals the total mass of the products.

Balanced equations

Chemical reactions can also be shown by **balanced equations** made up of chemical formulae. These must have the same numbers of each type of atom on either side of the equation. For example:

$$2H_2 + O_2 \longrightarrow 2H_2O$$

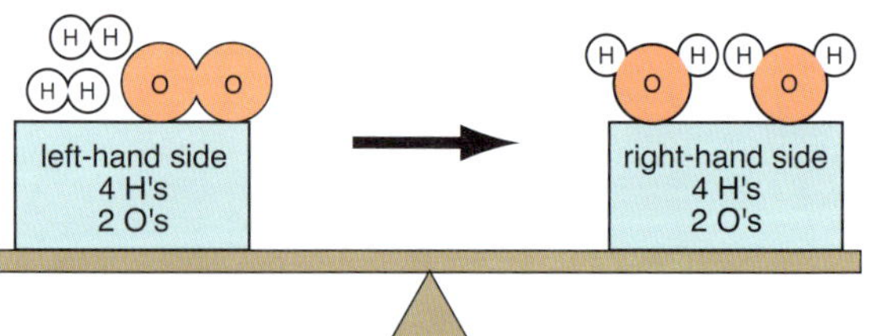

We can also include state symbols (s), (l), (g) or (aq).

Where:

s = solid
l = liquid
g = gas
aq = aqueous (dissolved in water)

For example:

$$2Na(s) + 2H_2O(l) \longrightarrow 2NaOH(aq) + H_2(g)$$

Answers: **1** hydrogen + chlorine → hydrogen chloride **2** $H_2(g) + Cl_2(g) \rightarrow 2HCl(g)$

D

H

Half equations in electrolysis

We can also write half equations to describe the reactions at each electrode during electrolysis. For example, during the electrolysis of molten copper chloride or copper chloride solution:

At the **cathode** (negative electrode) we get:

$$Cu^{2+} + 2e^{-} \longrightarrow Cu$$

AT THE CATHODE (–)

The copper ion is feeling blue. It's lost two electrons. But help is available at the cathode.

Copper's in the pink. It gets two electrons and changes from an ion to an atom.

Cathode

Here are some other examples of metal ions being **reduced** at the cathode during electrolysis of their molten salts. The metal ions **gain** electrons.

$$Na^{+} + e^{-} \longrightarrow Na$$

Sodium ions gain 1 electron to form sodium atoms.

$$Al^{3+} + 3e^{-} \longrightarrow Al$$

Aluminium ions each gain 3 electrons to form aluminium atoms.

More examples throughout ***Chemistry for You***, especially pages 22– 6, 105 and 115.

At the **anode** (positive electrode) we get:

$$2Cl^{-} - 2e^{-} \longrightarrow Cl_2$$

Two Cl^{-} ions each lose their extra electron and make a Cl_2 molecule

Anode

At the anode, negatively charged ions lose their extra electrons:

$$2O^{2-} - 4e^{-} \longrightarrow O_2$$

The negatively charged ions are **oxidised** at the anode.

Take care:

- Positive metal ions have to ***gain*** electrons at the cathode in order to change into metal atoms.
- At the anode, ***molecules*** of gas often form, such as O_2 or Cl_2, not atoms.

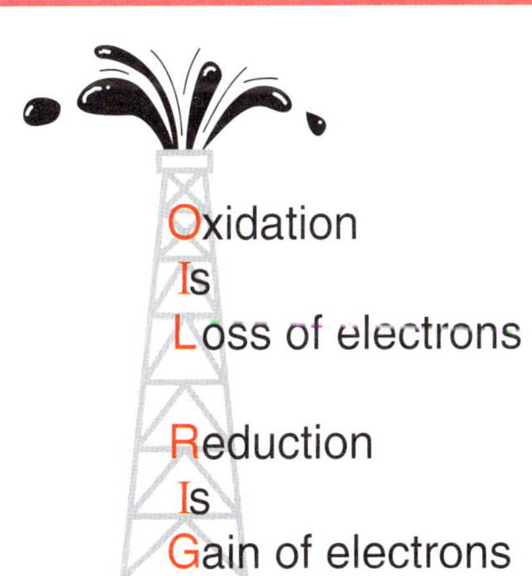

Examination Questions – Representing reactions

Year 11 questions

1 **Smelting with Carbon**

This question is about extracting metals from their compounds using the element carbon.

a) The reaction shown in the diagram can be used to extract a sample of metallic lead from lead oxide.

Carbon is more reactive than lead and therefore combines with the oxygen in the lead oxide. The carbon dioxide formed is given off leaving the lead behind.

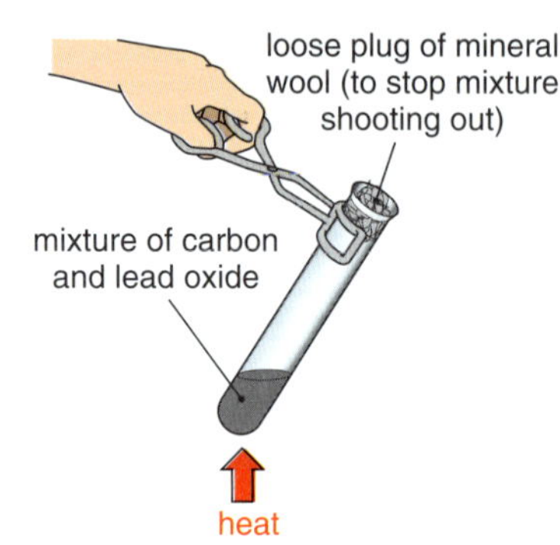

i Write a word equation to represent this reaction.

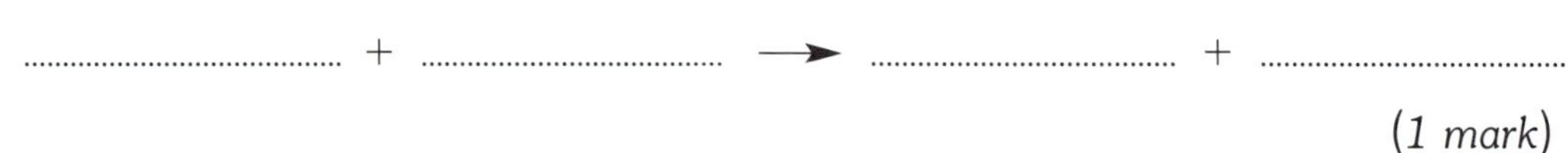

(1 mark)

ii A student performing this experiment decided to measure the mass of the reactants and products obtained. The results are shown below. One result is missing – use the three values given to work out what the fourth value should be.

Substance	mass/g
Lead oxide	446
Carbon	12

Substance	mass/g
Lead	414
Carbon dioxide	....

(1 mark)

b) A number of similar reactions are used in a blast furnace to extract iron from its ore.

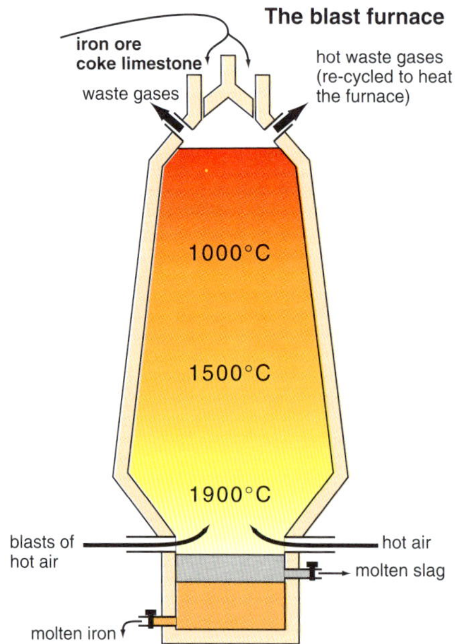

The reactions taking place in the blast furnace can be described as follows:

1. Carbon combines with oxygen to form carbon dioxide.
2. Carbon dioxide combines with carbon to form carbon monoxide.
3. Iron oxide is reduced by carbon monoxide to give iron and carbon dioxide.

i Write a word equation for reaction 2. Marks

.... + ... ⟶ ....

(1 mark)

ii The word equation for reaction 1 can be written as

carbon + oxygen ⟶ carbon dioxide

Give the symbol equation for this reaction (including state symbols).

.... + ... ⟶ ....

(2 marks)

iii A symbol equation for the main reduction reaction can be shown as follows:

$Fe_2O_3(s)$ + ... $CO(g)$ ⟶ ....$Fe(l)$ + ... $CO_2(g)$

The equation is not balanced. Add numbers in front of the symbols above to balance the equation.

(2 marks) 7

2 **Extraction by electrolysis**

This question is about using an electric current to obtain a sample of metal from one of its compounds.

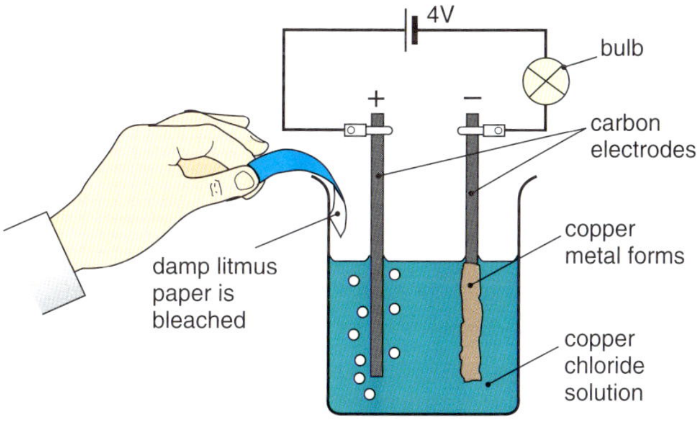

a) The electric current splits the copper chloride into its two constituent elements.

i Write a word equation to represent this reaction.

.... ⟶ .... + ...

(1 mark)

ii A word equation for the reaction at the cathode, by which copper metal forms, is given below:

copper ions + electrons ⟶ copper atoms

Write a balanced symbol equation for this change.

.... + ... ⟶ ....

(2 marks)

iii A symbol equation for the reaction taking place at the anode can be written as follows:

.... $Cl^-(aq)$ ⟶ .... $Cl_2(g)$ + ... e^-

Add numbers, where necessary, to the spaces in the equation in order to balance it.

(2 marks) 5

Getting the Grades – Structures and Bonding

Try this question, then compare your answer with the two examples opposite ▶

1 This question is about the forces which hold together the particles in a compound.

a) The diagram shows the arrangement of ions in a crystal of sodium chloride.

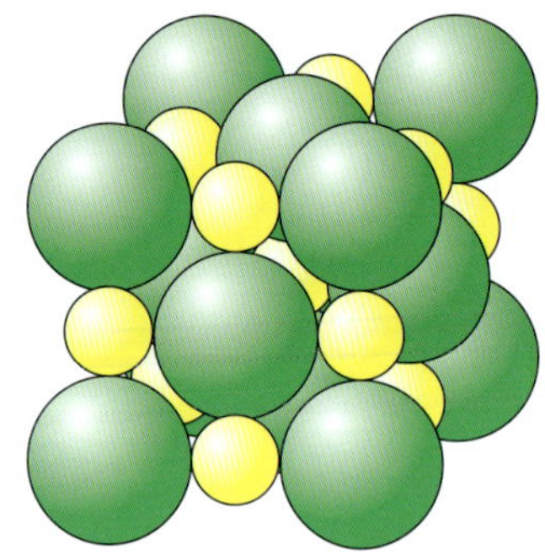

Use the list below to complete the following passage. Each word should be used once:

lattice, giant, ionic, sodium, chloride

A crystal of sodium chloride is formed as a result of the .... bonding which takes place between the positively charged .... ions and the negatively charged .... ions. The sodium ions are surrounded by chloride ions, and the chloride ions are then surrounded by sodium ions to form an interlocking .... ionic .... *(3 marks)*

b) Describe and explain the following two properties of sodium chloride:

i melting point

....

.... *(2 marks)*

ii solubility in water

....

.... *(2 marks)*

c) When melted or dissolved in water, sodium chloride will conduct an electric current. Explain, in terms of the behaviour of ions, why this is the case.

....

.... *(1 mark)*

d) One of the chlorides of carbon formed when chlorine atoms bond with carbon atoms is called tetracholoromethane. This compound has the formula CCl_4 and is composed of small molecules.

i Use the space below to draw a diagram to show the arrangement of electrons in a molecule of tetracholoromethane.

(2 marks)

ii Suggest **two** of the properties of tetracholoromethane.

....

.... *(2 marks)*

[Total 12 marks]

GRADE 'A' ANSWER

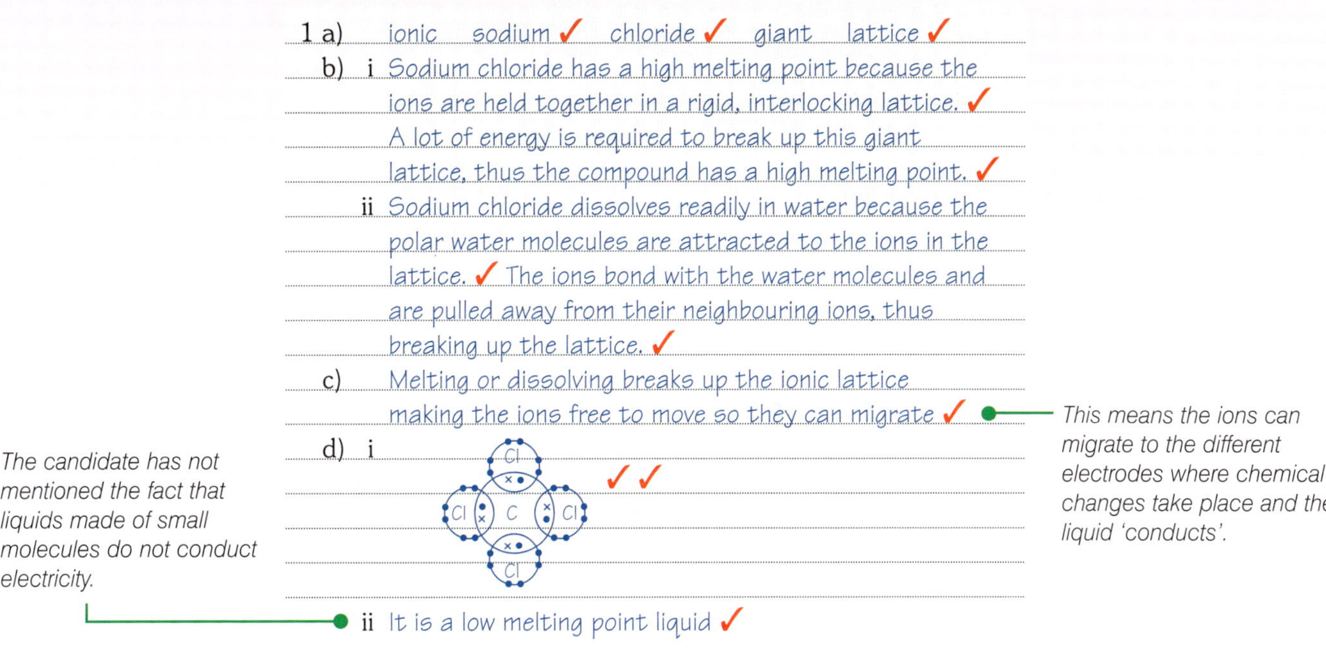

11 marks = Grade A answer

Improve your Grades A up to A*

Look up some of the properties of the oxides and chlorides of the elements of period 2 and period 3. Clear trends from ionic to covalent character can be seen in these substances and will help you to predict some of the properties of other compounds.
Take care to pick out giant structures as these will all have high melting points.

GRADE 'C' ANSWER

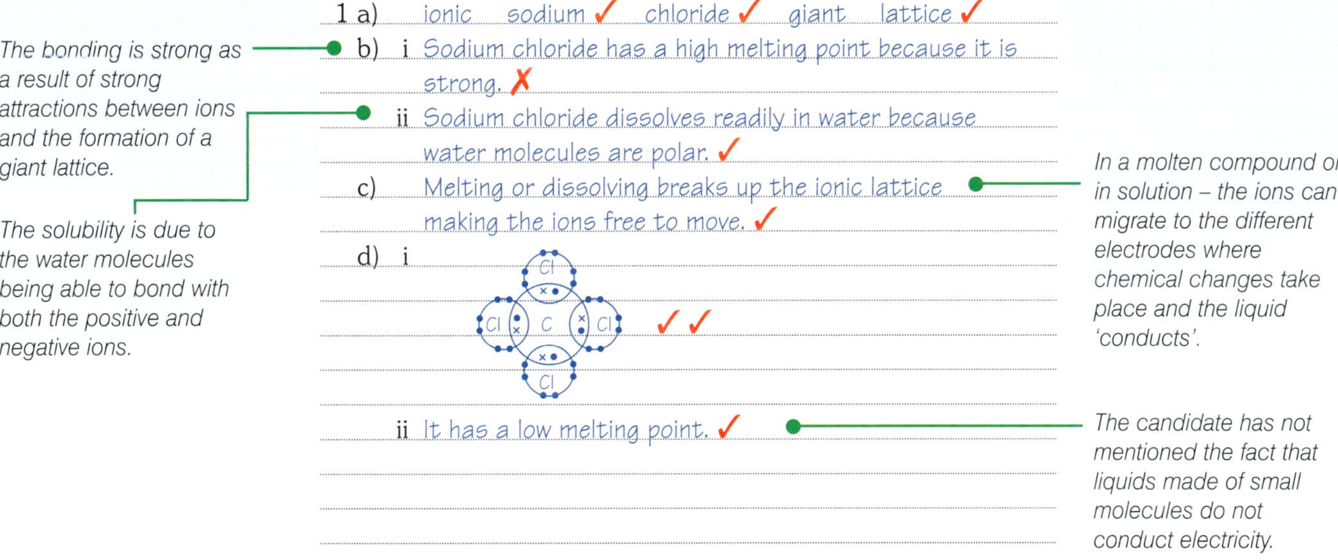

8 marks = Grade C answer

Improve your Grades C up to B

Use the periodic table to help you with your predictions of ionic or covalent character. Get a copy of the table and highlight: metals, giant lattices, small molecules. Note that high melting points are the result of a giant structure.

Remember: metals with non metals = ionic compounds,
and non metals with non metals = covalent compounds.

19 Aqueous chemistry

ThinkAbout:

1 What is the source of the energy that drives the water cycle?
2 What do we call the type of water that forms a scum with soap?
3 What is the main source of nitrate pollution in water?
4 Which statement is true:
A Most solids get more soluble in water as the temperature rises, but most gases get less soluble.
B Most solids get less soluble in water as the temperature rises, but most gases get more soluble.

The water cycle

Water is a good **solvent**. It forms **solutions** with many **solutes**.

The 'water cycle' shows how water moves around the Earth.

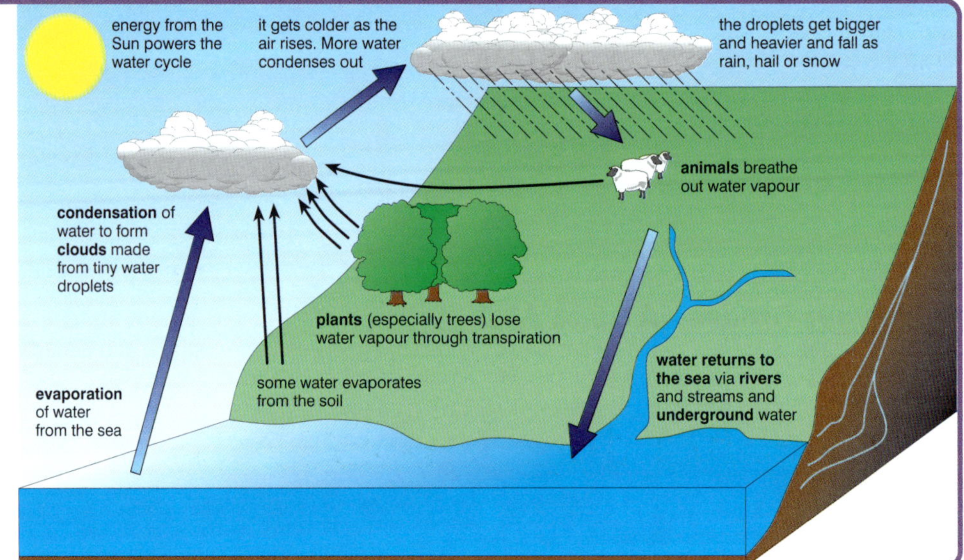

Hard water

Drinking water is purified by **physical** means (filter beds of sand and gravel to remove solids) and **chemical** means (chlorine to kill bacteria) before it reaches our taps.

Hard water contains dissolved **calcium** ions ($Ca^{2+}(aq)$) and/or **magnesium** ions ($Mg^{2+}(aq)$).

We can soften the water by **precipitating** these ions out of solution:

calcium ions(aq) + sodium carbonate(aq)
→ calcium carbonate(s) + sodium ions(aq)

Or we can soften hard water by passing it through an **ion exchange column**.

Soapless detergents, made from crude oil products, will form lather even in hard water.

Disadvantages of hard water	Advantages of hard water
Difficult to form lather with soap.	Some people prefer the taste.
Scum forms in a reaction which wastes soap.	Calcium in the water is good for children's teeth and bones.
Scale (a hard crust) forms inside kettles. This wastes energy when you boil your kettle.	Helps to reduce heart illness.
Hot water pipes 'fur up' on the inside. The scale formed can even block up pipes completely.	Some brewers like hard water for making beer.
	A coating of scale (limescale) inside copper or lead pipes stops poisonous salts dissolving into our water.

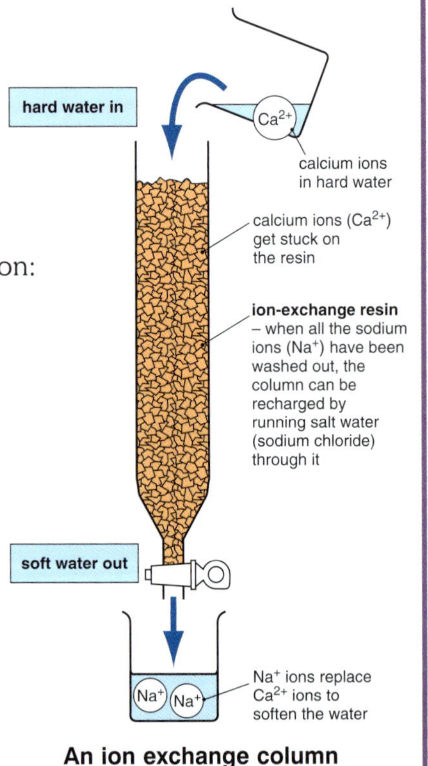

An ion exchange column

Water pollution

Water is also used as a **coolant** in industry. For example, it takes heat energy away from exothermic reactions in the Contact process used to manufacture sulphuric acid. It also transfers heat in power stations. If hot water that has been used as a coolant is pumped out into rivers it causes **thermal pollution** of the habitat. The delicate balance of nature is disturbed and aquatic life suffers. For example, the hotter the water, the less oxygen gas dissolves in it.

Rivers are also affected by fertilisers, detergents and sewage. Once dissolved into the water, algae thrive. When these die, micro-organisms in the river multiply rapidly as they feed on the dead algae. The micro-organisms use up the dissolved oxygen in the water so aquatic life dies. This problem is called **eutrophication**.

There are also worries about human health as nitrate fertilisers in drinking water are linked with stomach cancer and blue baby disease (where babies are deprived of oxygen).

Solubility curves

Unlike gases, the solubility of most solids increases as we raise the temperature. We can show this on solubility curves:

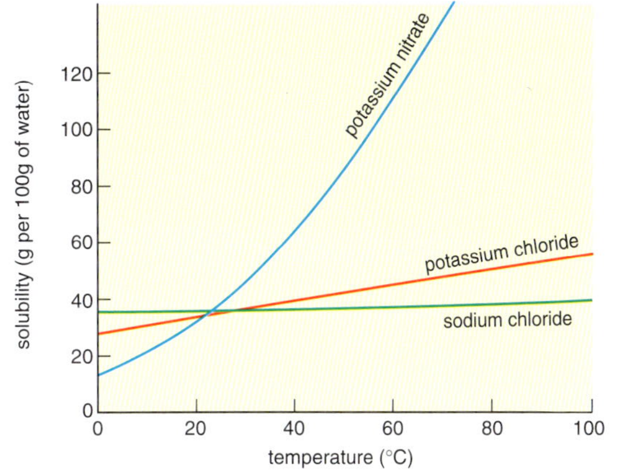

Water and acids

For acids to show their acidic properties, water must be present. This is because only when the acids are in solution, can their molecules split up (ionise) to form **H^+(aq) ions**. It is the H^+(aq) ions – protons surrounded by water molecules – that give an acidic solution its characteristic properties:

$$HCl(g) \longrightarrow H^+(aq) + Cl^-(aq)$$

Whereas excess H^+(aq) ions cause acidity in a solution, an excess of hydroxide ions, **OH^-(aq)**, cause a solution to be alkaline.

> Acids are said to be proton (H^+) **donors,** whereas bases are proton **acceptors**.

- If almost all the acidic molecules in a solution split up (**complete ionisation**), we call the acid a **strong acid**. Examples include hydrochloric acid, nitric acid and sulphuric acid.
- On the other hand, only a few of the molecules of **weak acids**, such as citric acid, ethanoic acid and carbonic acid, split up in a solution.

Therefore given solutions of equal concentration, a strong acid will have a lower pH value than a weak acid. The strong acid will also react faster than a weak acid, for example with magnesium ribbon, because there is a higher concentration of H^+(aq) ions in its solution.

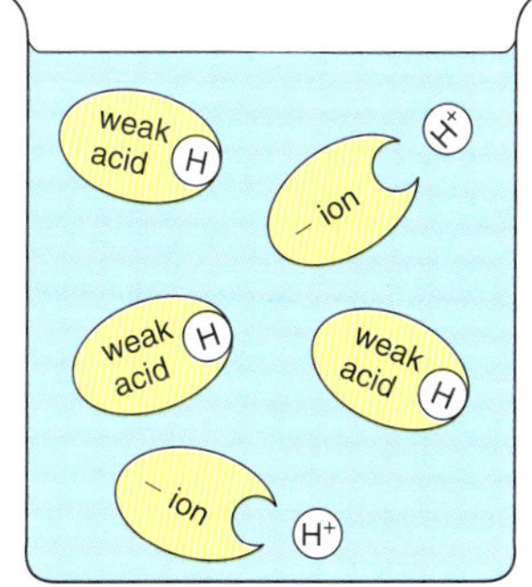

Solutions of weak acids contain 'undissociated' molecules in equilibrium with H^+ ions and negative ions

More in ***Chemistry for You,*** pages 149, 238, 250, 296–308.

Answers: **1** the Sun **2** hard water **3** nitrate fertilisers **4** A

Examination Questions – Aqueous chemistry

Year 11 questions

1 **Solubility curves**

The diagram opposite shows how the solubility of some solids varies as the temperature is changed.

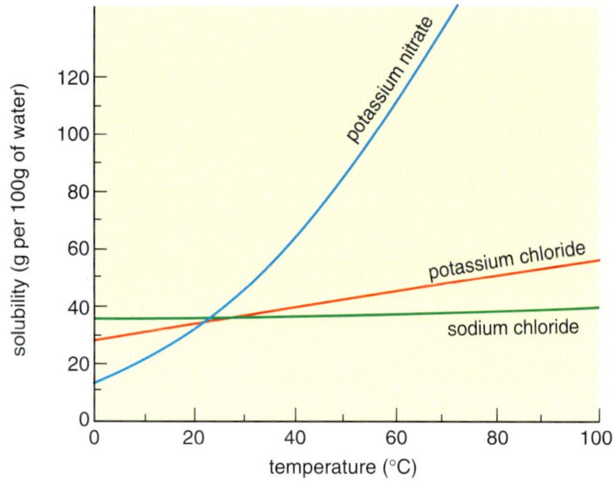

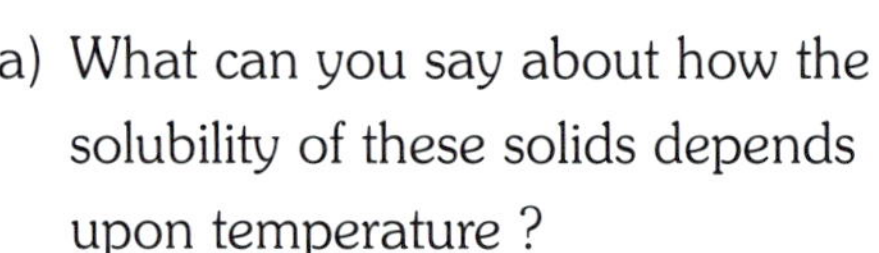

Marks

a) What can you say about how the solubility of these solids depends upon temperature ?

....

(*1 mark*)

b) What can you say about the effect temperature has upon the solubility of potassium nitrate compared with its effect on the solubility of sodium chloride?

....

....

(*2 marks*)

Use the data shown on the graph to answer the following questions:

c) i What mass of sodium chloride will dissolve in 100 g water 0°C?

.... (*1 mark*)

ii To what temperature would you need to raise 100 g water in order to dissolve 100 g potassium nitrate in it?

.... (*1 mark*)

iii If the solution produced in ii was cooled to 20°C, what would you expect to see in the tube?

.... (*1 mark*) 6

2 **Acids and water**

This question is about the differences between strong and weak acids

The diagrams show two test tubes, each containing a different acid.
Both acids are the same concentration. The same amount of magnesium ribbon was placed simultaneously in each tube.

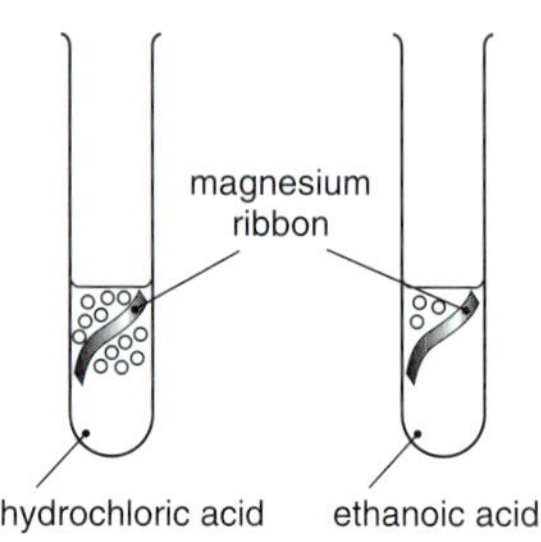

a) What difference can you see between the reactions in the two tubes?

.... (*1 mark*)

b) What does this reaction show about the reactivity of the two acids? Marks

.... (*1 mark*)

c) Explain, using ideas of dynamic equilibrium why this difference exists between the two acids.

....

....

(*2 marks*) 4

3 Hard water

This question is about impurities which are often present in some water supplies.

a) In some areas of the country the water which is supplied to homes and industry is described as 'hard' water.

Use the list below to complete the following passage. Each word should be used once:

calcium carbonate, carbonic acid, magnesium, soluble, calcium

Water which has either calcium or .... ions dissolved in it is described as hard water. This can form when a river flows over an area where the rock type is gypsum (which is calcium sulphate). This compound is slightly .... in water and so the .... ions get into the water.

Limestone (which is mainly ....) is not soluble in water but will dissolve due to the action of ...., formed when carbon dioxide in the atmosphere is dissolved in rainwater.

(*5 marks*)

b) Outline two of the disadvantages associated with hard water.

....

.... (*2 marks*)

c) What is meant by

i temporary hardness?

.... (*1 mark*)

ii permanent hardness?

.... (*1 mark*)

d) Explain one way in which permanent hardness can be removed from water.

....

....

....

.... (*2 marks*) 11

20

ThinkAbout:

1 Name the salt formed when these react:
   a) sodium hydroxide and dilute nitric acid
   b) magnesium and dilute sulphuric acid
   c) copper oxide and dil. hydrochloric acid.

2 Name these salts:
   a) $ZnCl_2$
   b) $Cu(NO_3)_2$
   c) K_2SO_4

Reactions that produce salts

As you saw in Topic 3, we get salts formed in reactions with acids.
Here are some examples of reactions that produce salts:

Acid and metal

acid + a metal ⟶ a salt + hydrogen

$H_2SO_4(aq) + Mg(s) \longrightarrow MgSO_4(aq) + H_2(g)$

- This method is for metals that are ***more reactive*** than hydrogen. It will not work with metals, such as copper, that can't displace hydrogen from the acidic solution.
- This method should not be used with highly reactive metals, such as sodium or potassium, because the reaction is too violent and will explode.

Acid and base

acid + a base (insoluble) ⟶ a salt + water

$H_2SO_4(aq) + CuO(s) \longrightarrow CuSO_4(aq) + H_2O(l)$

See page 17 for the method to use to prepare the salt formed.

Acid and alkali

acid + an alkali (a soluble base) ⟶ a salt + water

$HNO_3(aq) + KOH(aq) \longrightarrow KNO_3(aq) + H_2O(l)$

See titration on the next page for a suitable method to prepare the salt.

Precipitation reactions

This method is used when the salt you want to make is insoluble in water (see the table on page 104 for some examples), e.g.

barium chloride + sodium sulphate ⟶ barium sulphate (the precipitate) + sodium chloride

$BaCl_2(aq) + Na_2SO_4(aq) \longrightarrow BaSO_4(s) + 2\,NaCl(aq)$

By direct combination

You can react some metals directly with a non-metal to form some halide salts, e.g.

iron + chlorine ⟶ iron(III) chloride

$2Fe(s) + 3Cl_2(g) \longrightarrow 2FeCl_3(s)$

In these reactions the anhydrous salt is formed. There is no water present to form hydrated crystals.

Answers: **1** a) sodium nitrate b) magnesium sulphate c) copper(II) chloride **2** a) zinc chloride b) copper(II) nitrate c) potassium sulphate

Titrations

We can measure the volume of acid and alkali that neutralise each other using titration and a suitable indicator.

- The concentration of a solution is given in moles per dm^3 ($mol\ dm^{-3}$).
- We can work out how many moles are in a ***certain*** volume of a solution with a known concentration, using this equation:

  number of moles in a solution

  $$= \text{its concentration} \times \left(\frac{\text{volume of solution in cm}^3}{1000}\right)$$

- We can work out the concentration of ***unknown solutions*** using the technique of titration.
- The balanced equation tells us the ratio of the ***numbers of moles*** of reactants involved in the titration reaction. Then we can use the fact that concentrations are expressed in moles per dm^3 ($mol\ dm^{-3}$) to give the answer.

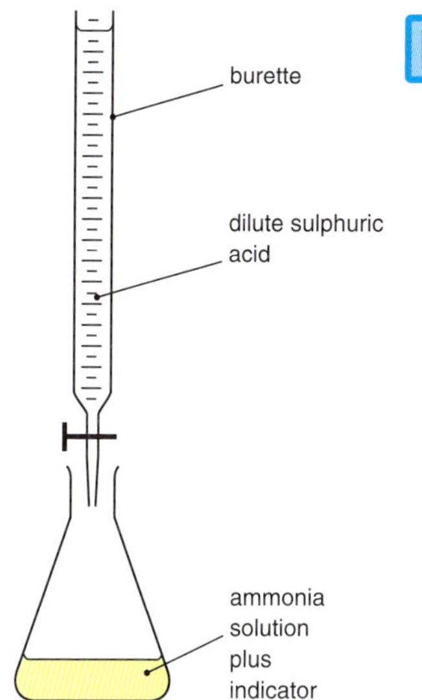

Titration using a burette

H

Example

10 cm^3 of 0.1 mol dm^{-3} hydrochloric acid is neutralised by 20 cm^3 of dilute sodium hydroxide. What is the concentration of the sodium hydroxide solution?
The equation for the neutralisation is:

$$NaOH(aq) + HCl(aq) \longrightarrow NaCl(aq) + H_2O(l)$$

- So 1 mole of hydrochloric acid reacts with 1 mole of sodium hydroxide.
- So in 20 cm^3 of the unknown sodium hydroxide solution, there must be the same number of moles as there are in 10 cm^3 of 0.1 mol dm^{-3} hydrochloric acid.
- Because we need twice the volume of sodium hydroxide, it must be half the concentration of the acid i.e. **0.05 mol dm^{-3}**.

You can prepare the salt made in a neutralisation reaction by:

- Repeating the titration without the indicator, adding just the right volume of acid.
- Heating the solution formed until the point of crystallisation.
- Then leaving the solution for a few days to let the remaining water evaporate off.

Read more in ***Chemistry for You***, pages 145, 150–1, 365.
(See the work of Arrhenius, Bronsted and Lowry.)

Examination Questions – Forming salts

Year 11 questions

1 **Soluble salts**

This question is about how you might use a neutralisation reaction to prepare a solid sample of the salt, sodium chloride.

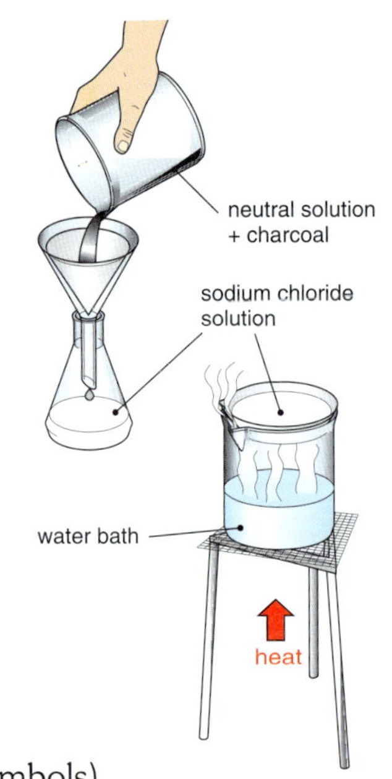

Marks

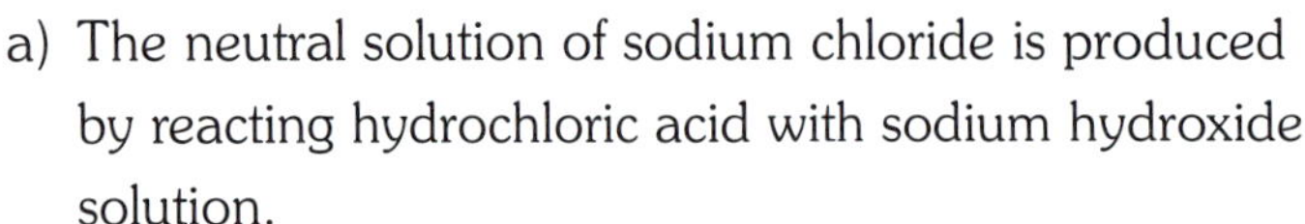

a) The neutral solution of sodium chloride is produced by reacting hydrochloric acid with sodium hydroxide solution.

hydrochloric acid + sodium hydroxide solution ⟶ sodium chloride + water

Write a symbol equation for this reaction (including state symbols).

.... *(2 marks)*

b) Give details of the procedure you would follow to obtain a neutral solution.

....

....

....

.... *(2 marks)*

c) What is the purpose of the charcoal used in this procedure?

.... *(1 mark)*

d) How does heating on a water bath help to produce crystals of salt?

.... *(1 mark)*

e) In following this procedure 10 cm^3 0.1 M hydrochloric acid was neutralised using 0.05 M sodium hydroxide solution. Show your workings clearly in your answers to the following questions.

i What volume of sodium hydroxide solution would be needed?

....

....

....

ii How many moles of sodium chloride would be produced?

....

....

iii What would the mass of this salt be?

(Relative atomic masses: Na = 23, Cl = 35.5)

....

.... *(4 marks)* 10

2 **Insoluble salts**

Marks

You will find the table of formulae of some common ions helpful in answering this question. (See page 117).

a) An insoluble salt can be prepared by mixing two solutions containing the two ions which make it up. This type of reaction is called a precipitation reaction.
For example

sodium chloride + silver nitrate ⟶ sodium nitrate + silver chloride

Reaction no.	Soluble salt 1	Soluble salt 2	Insoluble salt produced
1	sodium chloride	silver nitrate	silver chloride
2	sodium sulphate	barium chloride	
3	sodium iodide	lead nitrate	

Complete the table by writing the ***name*** of the insoluble salt produced in both cases.

(2 marks)

b) Write full symbol equations for:

i Reaction 2 ....

ii Reaction 3 ....

(4 marks)

c) Explain in detail how you would obtain a pure sample of the insoluble salt formed in reaction 3.

....

....

....

....

(3 marks) 9

3 **Insoluble base + Acid**

This question is about making a soluble salt from an insoluble oxide.

Study the diagram carefully.

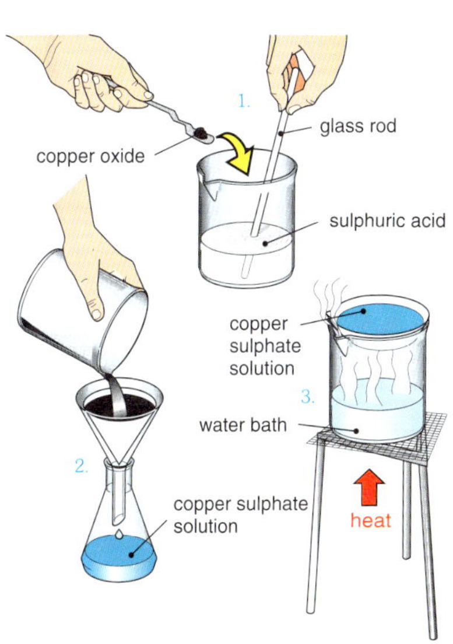

a) Write a full symbol equation for the reaction shown in the diagram.

.... *(1 mark)*

b) Use your own words to explain each step in the process shown:

1. ....

....

2. ....

....

3. ....

....

(3 marks) 4

21 ORGANIC CHEMISTRY

ThinkAbout:

1. How many covalent bonds can a carbon atom form?
2. How many covalent bonds can a hydrogen atom form?
3. Which type of reaction do we use to make alcoholic drinks?
4. What do we call the very large molecules made up from thousands of monomers?

Organic molecules

Organic compounds are based on carbon atoms (although they do not include oxides of carbon, carbonates or hydrogencarbonates). When we burn fossil fuels or wood in a good supply of air, this carbon is oxidised to carbon dioxide and any hydrogen gets oxidised to water. This is called a **combustion** reaction. When complete combustion takes place we get:

methane + oxygen ➝ carbon dioxide + water

If we only have a limited supply of air, we get incomplete combustion, and poisonous **carbon monoxide gas (CO)** is formed. This gas bonds to the **haemoglobin** in the blood and it can no longer carry oxygen around the body, leading to unconsciousness, then death.

We also get tiny solid particles of black carbon formed during incomplete combustion of fossil fuels and other organic compounds.

Isomers

H

Isomers are substances with the same chemical formula but ***different*** arrangements of atoms within their molecules.

Look at the isomers of C_4H_{10} below:

```
   H   H   H   H
   |   |   |   |
H—C—C—C—C—H
   |   |   |   |
   H   H   H   H
```

```
        H
        |
     H—C—H
   H    |    H
   |    |    |
H—C—C—C—H
   |    |    |
   H    H    H
```

Isomers with branching from their carbon chain have lower boiling points than their straight chain isomer. The more branching, the lower the boiling point (as branched chains cannot pack together as well as straight chains).

Groups of organic compounds

Groups or families of organic compounds that have the same general formula and undergo similar reactions are called **homologous series**. For example,

- The **alkanes** have the general formula $\mathbf{C_nH_{2n+2}}$.
- The **alkenes** (that contain one double bond) are $\mathbf{C_nH_{2n}}$.

All the alkenes undergo **addition reactions** (in which the double bond breaks and new single bonds form). For example:

$$C_2H_4 + H_2 \xrightarrow{\text{nickel catalyst}} C_2H_6$$

This reaction is used to harden unsaturated oils in the manufacture of margarine.

Alcohols

H

The homologous series of **alcohols** all contain the **—OH** grouping. This makes them more reactive than corresponding alkanes. The alcohols also have higher boiling points.

Answers: **1** four **2** one **3** fermentation **4** polymers

▶ **Ethanol** (C_2H_5OH) is a member of the alcohol family. It is used in alcoholic drinks, as a fuel and as a solvent.

We can make ethanol by two methods:

Fermenting glucose with yeast

The enzymes in yeast, in the absence of oxygen, break down the glucose:

glucose ⟶ ethanol + carbon dioxide

The carbon dioxide gas is allowed to escape, but no air is let in (otherwise the ethanol gets oxidised and tastes sour).

Hydrating ethene with steam

This is done under pressure in the presence of a phosphoric(V) acid catalyst:

ethene + steam ⟶ ethanol

- The ethanol produced by this second method can be run as a **continuous process** (as opposed to the batch process used in fermentation vats).
- However, the ethanol cannot be used in drinks.
- Also the process does use up a valuable resource in that crude oil is the raw material for ethene (whereas sugar is extracted from plants).

More in ***Chemistry for You***, pages 178–85.

▶ General reactions of alcohols

H

With sodium metal

alcohol + sodium ⟶ sodium salt of the alcohol + hydrogen

Combustion

alcohol + oxygen ⟶ carbon dioxide + water

Oxidation

alcohol ⟶ carboxylic acid

Esterification

alcohol + carboxylic acid $\xrightleftharpoons{\text{conc. sulphuric acid}}$ ester + water

Esters are used in perfumes and in food flavourings.

▶ More about polymers

H

There are two types of plastic:

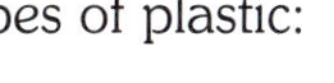

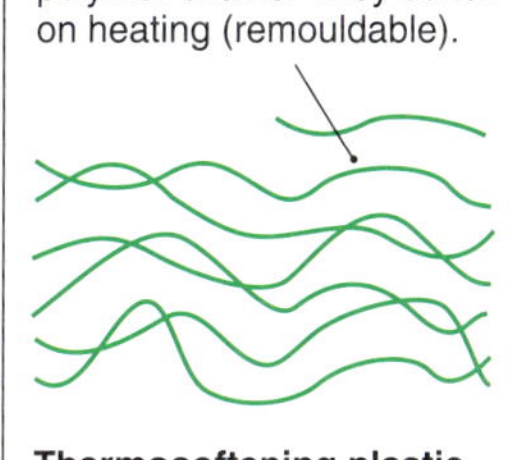

Thermosoftening plastic

Chains fixed together by strong covalent bonds. They can't be remoulded.

Thermosetting plastic

Burning plastics will reduce the volume of waste in landfill sites.

However, many plastics produce pollution if burned in a limited supply of air. Compounds containing chlorine form acidic hydrogen chloride gas, and those containing nitrogen give off toxic hydrogen cyanide gas.

Carboxylic acids

H

These are weak acids, found in citrus fruits and soft drinks (as citric acid) and in vinegar (as ethanoic acid). Aspirin is also a carboxylic acid (used to relieve pain and reduce the risk of heart attacks).

Here are the first three members of the homologous series:

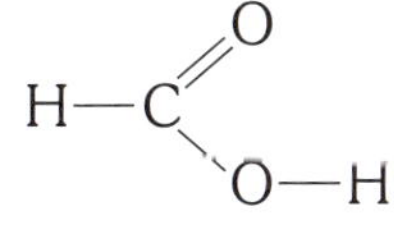

methanoic acid

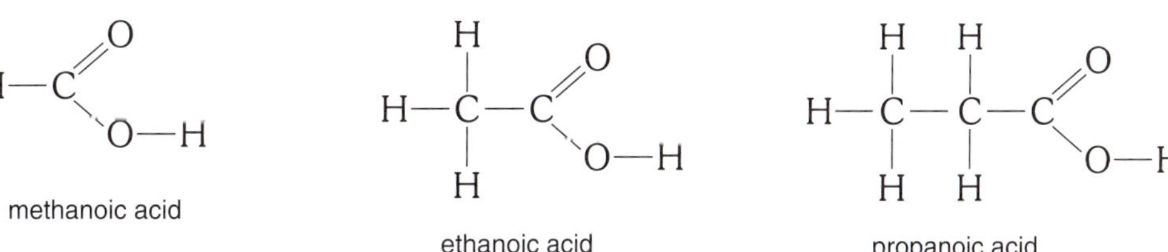

ethanoic acid

propanoic acid

They undergo the usual reactions of acids, for example:

ethanoic acid + sodium hydroxide ⟶ sodium ethanoate + water
(a salt of ethanoic acid)

ethanoic acid + sodium carbonate ⟶ sodium ethanoate + water + carbon dioxide

Examination Questions – Organic chemistry

1 **Alcohols**

This question is about the formation and reactions of an alcohol called ethanol. Ethanol has the formula C_2H_5OH.

Marks

a) Ethanol can be formed by the fermenting of glucose by yeast. The process produces a gas which will turn limewater cloudy.

i What is the gas produced as a result of the fermentation of glucose?

....

(1 mark)

ii Write a word equation to represent the fermentation process.

.... $\xrightarrow{\text{yeast}}$ .... + ...

(1 mark)

b) Ethanol can also be made by reacting ethene gas $C_2H_4(g)$ with steam in the presence of a catalyst of phosphoric(V) acid.

Write a symbol equation for this reaction.

.... + ... $\xrightarrow{\text{(catalyst of phosphoric acid)}}$ ....

(2 marks)

c) What is the advantage of producing ethanol

i from ethene?

....

ii by the fermentation of sugar?

....

(2 marks)

d) The ethanol produced by either method can be used in a variety of ways. Excluding alcoholic drinks, give two uses for ethanol.

....

....

(2 marks) 8

2 **Isomers**

This question is about isomers.

a) The two molecules drawn on the next page are isomers of the alkane, butane.

i Which of these two isomers will have the higher boiling point?

....

Marks

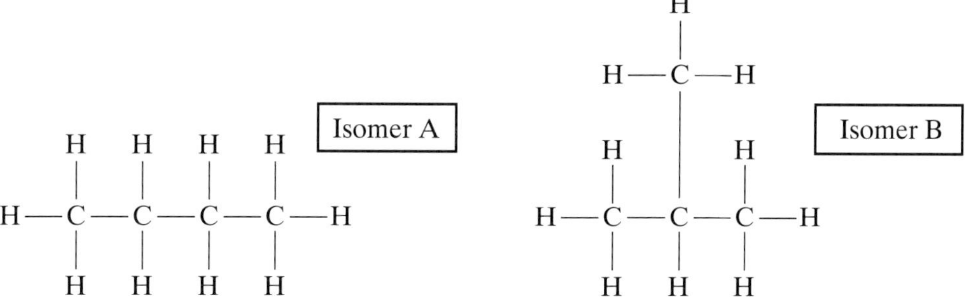

ii Explain your answer to i.

....

....

(3 marks)

b) How will the chemical properties of these two isomers differ? Explain your answer.

....

.... (2 marks) 5

3 **Carboxylic acids**

This question is about carboxylic acids are formed when an alcohol is oxidised.

a) Complete the table below to give the name and formula of each carboxylic acid formed when ethanol and propan-1-ol are oxidised.

Alcohol	**Formula**	**Name of carboxylic acid**	**Formula of carboxylic acid formed**
Methanol	CH_3OH	Methanoic acid	HCOOH
Ethanol	C_2H_5OH		
Propan-1–ol	C_3H_7OH		

(4 marks)

b) How will these acids react with:

i magnesium ribbon? ....

....

ii sodium carbonate solution? ....

.... (2 marks)

c) These acids will all react with alcohols in the presence of an acid catalyst to make sweet smelling compounds?

i What is the name for this class of sweet smelling compounds?

....

ii Write a word equation to show the general reaction by which these compounds are made.

.... + ... ⟶ .... + ...

(2 marks)

d) What can these compounds be used for?

....

(2 marks) 10

22 Industrial processes

▶ ThinkAbout:

1 What is the chemical symbol of:
a) aluminium b) magnesium
c) iron d) titanium?

2 What is the chemical formula of:
a) sulphur dioxide b) sulphur trioxide
c) sulphuric acid d) vanadium(V) oxide?

▶ Manufacture of sulphuric acid

Sulphuric acid (H_2SO_4) is manufactured in the **Contact process.**

- First of all, sulphur is burned in air to give sulphur dioxide gas (SO_2).
- Then sulphur dioxide is mixed with more air to yield sulphur trioxide in a reversible reaction.
- A compromise temperature of 450 °C is chosen and the gases are passed through layers of vanadium(V) oxide catalyst (V_2O_5).
- Finally, sulphur trioxide is added to concentrated sulphuric acid making fuming sulphuric acid, which is called **oleum**. Water is carefully added to the oleum to make 98% sulphuric acid.

In effect the reaction is:

$$SO_3(g) + H_2O(l) \longrightarrow H_2SO_4(l)$$

However, if this reaction were to be carried out as shown in the equation, a mist of sulphuric acid forms that is difficult to condense and would pollute the atmosphere.

▶ Some uses of sulphuric acid

Sulphuric acid is used to make **fertilisers** and **detergents**. It is the acid found inside **car batteries**.

Sulphuric acid is also a **dehydrating agent**. This means that it can remove H_2O from molecules in a chemical reaction with some compounds, for example:

sugar ⟶ carbon + water

hydrated copper sulphate *(blue crystals)* ⟶ anhydrous copper sulphate *(white powder)* + water

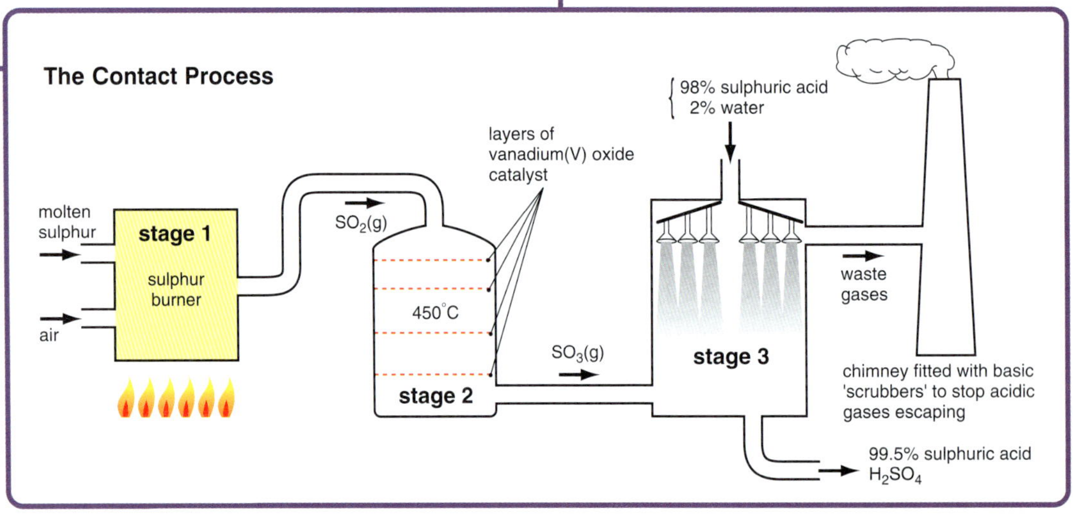

Answers: **1** a) Al b) Mg c) Fe d) Ti **2** a) SO_2 b) SO_3 c) H_2SO_4 d) V_2O_5

Anodising aluminium

Aluminium is quite a reactive metal, yet it resists corrosion. The thin oxide layer that coats aluminium protects it from attack by air and water.

We can improve aluminium's resistance to corrosion even further by making the oxide layer thicker. In industry this is done by **anodising** the aluminium.

- The first step is to remove the existing layer of aluminium oxide. This is done by dipping the aluminium into sodium hydroxide solution.
- The exposed aluminium is made the **anode** in the electrolysis of dilute sulphuric acid:

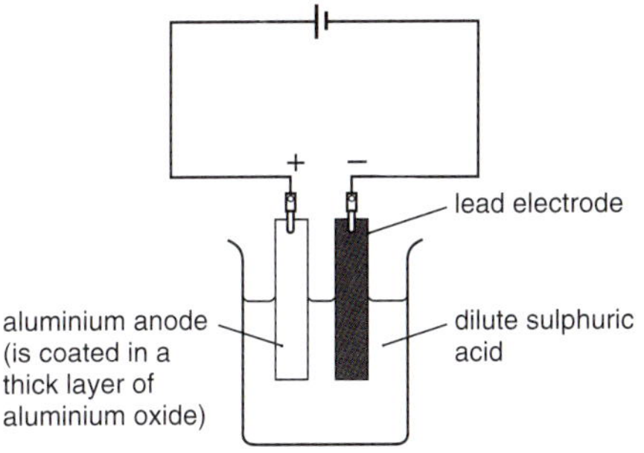

- The oxygen gas made reacts with the aluminium anode. It makes a thicker, protective layer of aluminium oxide.

Steel making

Iron from the blast furnace contains impurities. Most of these are removed when converting this iron into steel. Oxygen gas is blown over a molten mixture of iron (which includes scrap iron). The impurities get oxidised and are released as gases or removed as slag (formed by adding lime).

There are different types of steel depending on the amount of carbon left in it:

- **High carbon steels** are strong but brittle.
- Whereas **mild steel** (containing less carbon) makes a softer steel that is easy to press into shapes, for example in car bodies.
- **Alloy steels** are made by mixing other metals into the molten steel.

Electroplating metals

Most metals can be coated with a layer of another metal in an electrolysis cell:

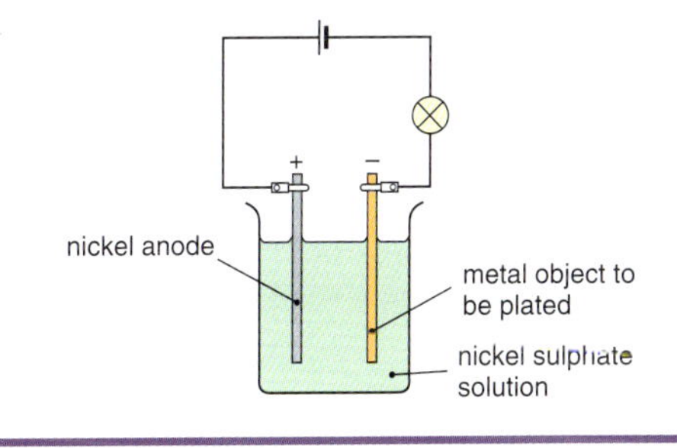

Extracting titanium

We find titanium in many alloys mixed with other metals. It is used to make low density alloys that can withstand high temperatures. These alloys also resist corrosion. They are used in the aircraft industry, for example, to make the turbines in jet engines.

Titanium is a metal of 'medium' reactivity, so in theory we could use carbon to extract it. However, titanium carbide would be formed which spoils the useful properties of the metal.

Therefore, we use a ***more reactive metal*** to extract the titanium. In industry sodium or magnesium are used as the reducing agent.

This is the way we extract titanium from its ore:

- Titanium dioxide (TiO_2, rutile) is separated from the ore called ilmenite, which also contains iron oxide, using magnets.
- Titanium dioxide is changed into titanium(IV) chloride ($TiCl_4$):

$$TiO_2(s) + C(s) + 2Cl_2(g) \xrightarrow{\text{heat}} TiCl_4(g) + CO_2(g)$$

- The products are cooled down and titanium(IV) chloride condenses to a liquid. It is purified by distilling it.
- The titanium(IV) chloride is reduced by sodium in an atmosphere of argon:

$$TiCl_4(g) + 4Na(l) \xrightarrow{\text{heat}} Ti(s) + 4NaCl(l)$$

- The molten sodium chloride (or magnesium chloride) is tapped off.

More in ***Chemistry for You,*** pages, 92, 94, 97, 108, 114 and 154–5.

Examination Questions – Industrial processes

1 **Sulphuric acid**

This question is about the process by which the element sulphur is turned into sulphuric acid. The first stage in the process is the burning of sulphur in air to give sulphur dioxide:

a) Write a word equation for this reaction. Marks

.... + ... → ....

(2 marks)

b) The sulphur dioxide SO_2 is then turned into sulphur trioxide SO_3 by heating it with more oxygen in the presence of a vanadium(V) oxide catalyst. The equation for this reaction is shown below.

i Put numbers in front of the formulae, where necessary, to balance it.

..............................$SO_2(g)$ + ...$O_2(g)$ $\rightleftharpoons$ ....$SO_3(g)$

ii What does the $\rightleftharpoons$ symbol mean?

....

(3 marks)

c) The final reaction involves the addition of water to the sulphur trioxide in order to make sulphuric acid.
Write a symbol equation for this reaction.

....

(2 marks)

d) What is the sulphuric acid produced then used for?

....

....

(2 marks) 9

2 **Extracting Titanium**

Titanium is one of the transition metals and a metal of medium reactivity. It is extracted from its oxide, TiO_2. Several stages are involved in the process

a) Why is titanium such a useful metal?

....

(1 mark)

b) The extraction process is described below.
Use words from the list to complete the passage:

reduced, chlorine, carbon, cooled, distillation

Titanium dioxide is separated from the ore called ilmenite, which also contains iron oxide, using magnets. The TiO_2 is heated with .... *and* ....
This produces titanium chloride and carbon dioxide gas. The products are then .... *and the titanium chloride condenses to a liquid. This liquid is purified by* .... *The titanium chloride is then* .... *by sodium metal in an atmosphere of argon.* (3 marks)

c) An equation for the last stage in this process is given below: Marks

$$\ldots\ TiCl_4(g) + \ldots\ Na(l) \longrightarrow \ldots\ Ti(s) + \ldots\ NaCl(l)$$

i Put numbers in front of the formulae, where necessary, in order to balance the equation.

ii Explain why this reaction can be regarded as a redox reaction.

....

....

(4 marks) 8

3 **Making steel**

This question is about the way in which iron from the blast furnace is converted to steel.

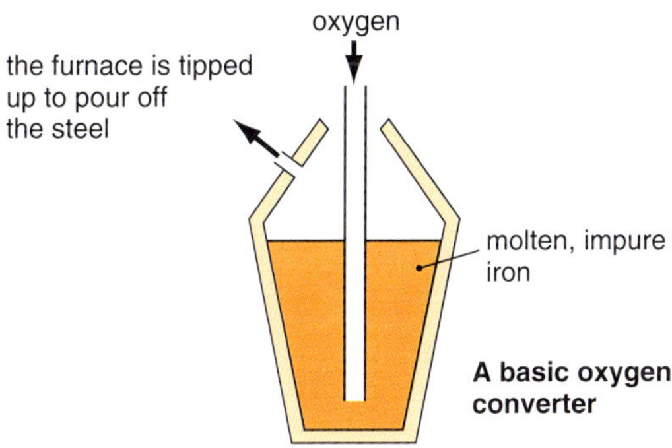

In this process oxygen is blown through the molten iron. Carbon is one of the impurities.

a) i How does the oxygen remove carbon from the iron?

....

....

ii Write an equation to represent this reaction.

....

(3 marks)

b) Other metals might be added to the molten iron at this point to make alloys.

i What is an alloy?

....

ii Why are alloys useful?

....

(3 marks) 6

23 Detection and identification

▶ ThinkAbout:

1. Do the atoms of metals form positively or negatively charged ions?
2. What is the formula of an aluminium ion (Al is in Group 3 in the Periodic Table)?
3. Name three halide ions.
4. What is the charge on a sulphate ion?
5. Give the formula of:
   a) ammonium sulphate b) iron(III) nitrate.

▶ Identifying negatively charged ions (anions)

Here is a summary of the tests we can use to identify some common negatively charged ions (anions):

Anion	Test
Chloride (Cl^-)	Dissolve in dilute nitric acid, then a white precipitate forms with silver nitrate solution. (The precipitate of silver chloride dissolves in dilute ammonia solution.)
Bromide (Br^-) **H**	Dissolve in dilute nitric acid, then a cream precipitate forms with silver nitrate solution. (The precipitate of silver bromide is insoluble in dilute ammonia solution, but dissolves in concentrated ammonia solution.)
Iodide (I^-) **H**	Dissolve in dilute nitric acid, then a pale yellow precipitate forms with silver nitrate solution. (The precipitate of silver iodide is insoluble in both dilute and concentrated ammonia solutions.)
Sulphate (SO_4^{2-})	Dissolve in dilute hydrochloric acid, then a white precipitate of barium sulphate forms with barium chloride solution.
Nitrate (NO_3^-) **H**	Add sodium hydroxide solution and heat, then test the gas given off (ammonia) with damp red litmus paper, which turns blue.
Carbonate (CO_3^{2-})	Add dilute acid, then pass the carbon dioxide gas through limewater, which turns milky (cloudy).

▶ Identifying positively charged ions (cations)

Here are the positive ions (cations) we can test with sodium hydroxide solution:

Cation	Result of adding sodium hydroxide solution
Copper(II)	Pale blue precipitate
Iron(II)	Dirty green precipitate
Iron(III)	Rusty brown precipitate
Aluminium	White precipitate which dissolves in excess sodium hydroxide
Magnesium	White precipitate
Calcium	White precipitate

▶ Flame tests

Some metal ions also give out coloured light when we heat them in a Bunsen flame:

Cation	Colour of flame test
Sodium	Bright yellow
Lithium	Red (scarlet)
Calcium	Brick red
Potassium	Lilac
Barium	Apple green

H

▶ Ammonium ions (NH_4^+) give off ammonia gas when we heat them with sodium hydroxide solution. Ammonia is the only common alkaline gas – we test for ammonia with damp pink litmus paper: it turns blue.

Answers: **1** positively charged ions **2** Al^{3+} **3** fluoride / chloride / bromide / iodide **4** 2− **5** a) $(NH_4)_2SO_4$ b) $Fe(NO_3)_3$

Instrumental analysis

Nowadays we can use modern instruments to detect and measure very small amounts of elements and compounds in samples. These machines are used to monitor and control water quality, but have also found many other uses, for example in forensic science and in hospitals. Here is one machine we use to detect unknown elements (in, say, a sample of water being analysed) and one that detects unknown compounds.

Atomic spectrometers

Spectrometers are expensive machines that analyse the energy (in the form of electromagnetic radiation, such as light) absorbed or given out by a sample. Atomic spectrometers are used to detect which elements are in a sample. The sample is heated in a flame. Any molecules are broken down at this stage. The energy from the flame causes electrons in the atoms of the sample to jump into higher energy levels (shells). When the electrons fall back to lower energy levels they give out energy.

The energy given out is called the **emission spectrum** of the element. Each element has its own characteristic set of energies that it gives out. We can see these as lines in a spectrum or as peaks when analysed by a detector and fed into a computer.

This method can be used to tell us which elements are present by matching the emission spectrum to a database of known elements stored on the computer. It can also show how much of each element is present. For example, we can now detect toxic mercury in a sample of water down to traces as low as 0.000 000 001 g!

Atomic spectrometers are used in other industries, besides the water industry, to monitor samples. For example, the steel industry can carefully analyse the amounts of trace elements present in steel to control its quality.

Visible–ultraviolet spectrophotometers

These instruments are used to analyse which compounds are present in a sample. The sample is not broken up by any harsh treatment in the machine, such as heating it in a flame. Light is shone on the sample, then the result is analysed to see which wavelengths are absorbed.

The spectrum can be matched or 'fingerprinted' against known samples and then the sample identified.

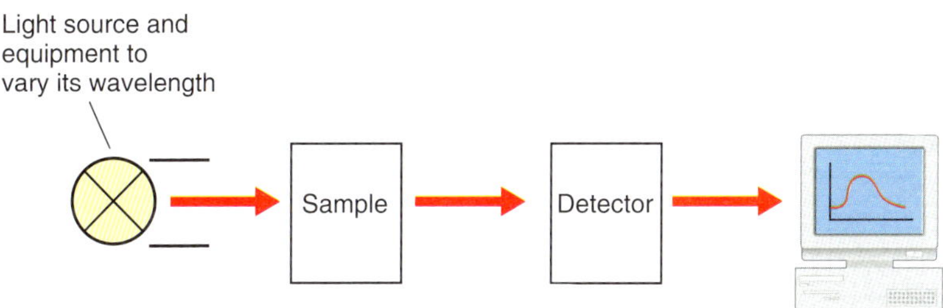

If a compound does not absorb light in the visible–ultraviolet part of the spectrum, this technique will not work. However, the compound can be reacted with other compounds to give products that do absorb light in the right range. Then these compounds can be detected. This method is used in the water industry to analyse levels of nitrate and phosphate pollutants in water supplies.

Two tell-tale carbonates

- You can recognise **copper carbonate** because it turns from green to black (forming copper oxide) when heated.
- Heating **zinc carbonate** turns the white powder bright yellow. Then it goes white again when cool. It forms zinc oxide, when heated, which is responsible for the colour change.

More in ***Chemistry for You,*** pages 152–3, 309–11.

Examination Questions – Detection and identification

1 **Precipitation reactions**

When samples of certain solutions are mixed – a precipitate is sometimes produced.

This type of reaction can be used to identify unknown salts in solution.

Marks

a) What is a precipitate?

....

....

(*2 marks*)

b) When silver nitrate solution is added to a solution of sodium chloride, a white precipitate is produced.

i Write a word equation for this reaction.

....

ii What is the name of the white precipitate?

....

iii This reaction is used to test for a particular type of ion. Which ion?

....

(*4 marks*)

c) When sodium chloride is subjected to a flame test, it gives a particular colour.

i Describe how to perform a flame test.

....

....

ii What colour would the flame be in this case?

....

(*3 marks*) 9

2 **Unknown compound**

This question is about using chemical tests to identify the chemical composition of a white powder.

The white powder was dissolved in nitric acid. The solution produced was then tested:

Test	**Result**
Flame test	Lilac flame
Barium chloride solution added	White precipitate produced

a) What is the metal ion (cation) in the white powder?

.... (*1 mark*)

b) What is the negatively charged ion (anion) in the white powder?

.... (*1 mark*)

c) What is the formula of the white powder?

.... (*1 mark*)

d) Write a balanced symbol equation for the reaction between the solution of the unknown salt and the barium chloride solution. Marks

....

(2 marks) 5

3 Identification

The passage below describes the changes which took place when a sample of copper carbonate was treated in a variety of ways. The results of each test have been omitted from the passage. Use the words from the list to complete the passage:

pale blue, colourless, green, black, white

a) *Reaction 1.* *When a sample of copper carbonate was heated in a test tube, its colour changed from a .... powder to copper oxide which is a .... powder. Carbon dioxide gas was given off in this process. This gas was identified by the fact that it produced a .... precipitate when bubbled through limewater.*

Reaction 2. *When dilute acid was added to a sample of the copper carbonate, bubbles of .... gas were produced.*

Reaction 3. *The copper oxide produced in 1 was added to dilute nitric acid until no more would dissolve. Excess copper oxide was then filtered out. The resultant solution was tested by the addition of sodium hydroxide solution. This reacted with the metal ions present, to produce a .... precipitate.* (3 marks)

b) Reaction 1.

Write a word equation for this reaction.

.... → .... + ...

What sort of reaction is this ?

.... (2 marks)

c) Reaction 2.

In this reaction, a lot of visible changes took place. Use the space below to describe all the changes you would see as it progresses.

....

....

.... (2 marks)

d) Reaction 3.

The reaction between copper oxide and nitric acid produced a solution of a salt called copper nitrate.

This can be represented as:

copper oxide + nitric acid → copper nitrate + water

i What is the name given to this type of reaction where an acid reacts with the oxide of a metal?

....

ii Write a balanced symbol equation for this reaction.

.... (3 marks) 10

Examination answers and tips 

TOPIC 1. Metals in the periodic table

Year 10 questions

1 Iron 2
Magnesium 3
Mercury 1
Potassium 4

2 Conduct 1
Corrode 3
Cut 2
Melt 4

3 It bends and shapes easily
It is a good conductor of electricity

Year 11 questions

1 a) He arranged the elements in order of increasing relative atomic masses.
b) These three elements had similar properties and so they were put in the same group (column).

Examiner's Tip ✓
Note that the question asks specifically about the way in which Mendeleev organised his periodic table. Electronic configurations and some elements were at that time yet to be discovered. Mendeleev left spaces for unknown elements and he was also bold enough to change the order of some elements' atomic masses so that elements with similar chemical properties could be grouped vertically.

c) i The elements are arranged in order of increasing atomic (proton) number.
ii Moving from left to right (sodium to argon) the number of electrons in the atoms increases by one for each element.
Thus an argon atom has 7 more electrons than an atom of sodium. **5**

Examiner's Tip ✓
Remember, the extra electrons are all in the same outer shell. On moving to the next period, a new outer shell is formed.

TOPIC 2. Useful products from metal ores

Year 10 questions

1 Electrolysis 1
Neutralisation 4
Oxidation 3
Thermal decomposition 2

2 Metal K 4 Metal L 3
Metal M 1 Metal N 2

Year 11 questions

1 a) 70 % of the ore is iron oxide. Thus in 2000 tonnes (of ore) the amount (mass) of iron oxide is

$$\left(\frac{2000}{100}\right) \times 70 = 1400 \text{ tonnes}$$

b) Formula of iron oxide is Fe_2O_3
The formula mass of iron oxide is
$(2 \times 56) + (3 \times 16) = 160$

The proportion of iron in iron oxide is $\frac{112}{160}$

Thus the mass of iron that can be extracted from 1400 tonnes iron oxide is thus $\left(\frac{112}{160}\right) \times 1400$

$= 980$ tonnes **4**

Examiner's Tip ✓
Be sure to use the mass of iron oxide (1400 tonnes) and not the mass of ore (2000 tonnes) for the calculation involving formula masses. If the answer to part a) was wrong, you would still get marks in part b), providing the calculation was correct and workings were shown in b).

2 a) Ionic compounds have high melting points because the oppositely charged ions are attracted strongly to one another, and a rigid three dimensional lattice is formed as a result.

Examiner's Tip ✓
In ionic bonding, the ions of one charge, attract oppositely charged ions in all directions. So positive ions are surrounded by negative ions which are surrounded by positive ions and so on. Therefore a lot of forces hold an ionic solid together. This makes it difficult to separate ions in these giant structures so ionic compounds have high melting points.

b)

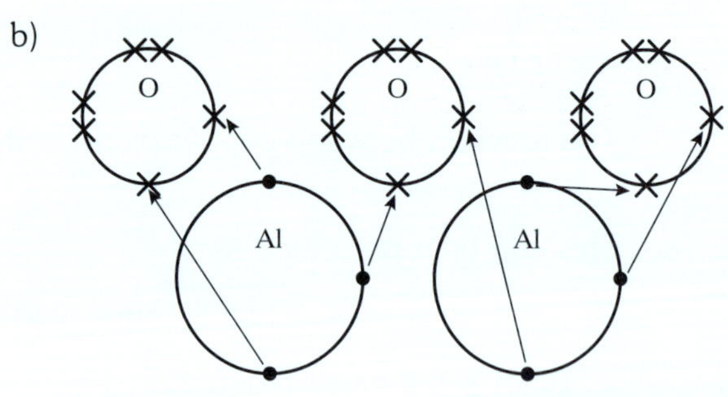

c) $Al^{3+} + \mathbf{3}\,e^- \longrightarrow Al$

Examiner's Tip ✓
In this process, the aluminium ions are reduced to aluminium atoms at the cathode.

TOPIC 3. Acids, alkalis and salts

Year 10 questions

1 Ammonia
Sodium hydroxide

> ***Examiner's Tip*** ✓
> *Iron hydroxide is insoluble in water.*

2 2.1 C
2.2 B
2.3 A
2.4 C

Year 11 questions

1 a) i Solution B
ii Solution D
iii Solution A

> ***Examiner's Tip*** ✓
> *Remember that strongly acidic solutions have low pH values.*

i neutral
ii Neutralisation
iii A salt and water **6**

> ***Examiner's Tip*** ✓
> *A helpful general equation to remember:*
> *acid + alkali ⟶ a salt + water*

TOPIC 4. Useful products from rocks

Year 10 questions

1 1.1 D
1.2 A
1.3 B
1.4 C

2 2 Cement mixed with sand and crushed rock
4 Concrete produced
1 Limestone heated in a kiln with clay
3 Water added to mixture **8**

3 A

4 C

TOPIC 5. Useful products from oil

Year 10 questions

1 Hydrocarbons with small molecules 4
The hydrocarbons are heated 1
The hydrocarbons are in a vapour state 2
Thermal decomposition of hydrocarbons 3

2 2.1 C
2.2 A
2.3 D
2.4 A

Year 11 questions

1 a) Alkanes are compounds whose molecules are composed of atoms of hydrogen and carbon only. All the bonds in an alkane are single bonds. Each carbon atom bonds to four other atoms, and each hydrogen atom bonds to only one carbon atom. The number of hydrogen atoms in a given alkane molecule will therefore depend upon the number of carbon atoms in the molecule – this is qiven by the formula C_nH_{2n+2}

> ***Examiner's Tip*** ✓
> *The Alkanes are a 'family' of compounds which share the same general formula. Knowing the number of carbon atoms (n) enables you to work out the molecular formula for any particular alkane.*

b) Polymerisation takes place when thousands of small, reactive molecules (monomers) join up with one another to form a large molecule (polymer). Therefore a polymer is made up of a large number of identical repeating units. **5**

> ***Examiner's Tip*** ✓
> *Remember – 'poly' means 'many'. A polymer molecule is often represented using a formula and square brackets to represent the repeating unit: Eg poly(ethene) is represented by:* $\left[CH_2\ CH_2 \right]_n$

TOPIC 6. Changes to the atmosphere

Year 10 questions

1 It is released during thermal decomposition of carbonate rocks
It reacts in seawater to form calcium carbonate

2 2.1 A
2.2 C
2.3 C
2.4 D

3 Carbon dioxide 4
Oxygen 3
Sulphur dioxide 2
Water vapour 1

Year 11 questions

1 a) i The amount of carbon dioxide released into the atmosphere has increased rapidly in recent times.
ii People are burning far more fossil fuels nowadays.

b) Carbon dioxide is a greenhouse gas that will contribute towards global warming. **4**

TOPIC 7. The rock record

Year 10 questions

1 Rock type A 2
Rock type B 4
Rock type C 1
Rock type D 3

2 2.1 D
2.2 D
2.3 A
2.4 A

3 Fossils 1
Plates 4
Rocks 2
Shapes 3

Year 11 questions

1 The outer layer of the Earth is made up of (tectonic) plates which are still moving.

TOPIC 8. Rates of reaction

Year 11 questions

1 a) There will be a steeper curve initially, which levels off at the same point (volume of hydrogen).

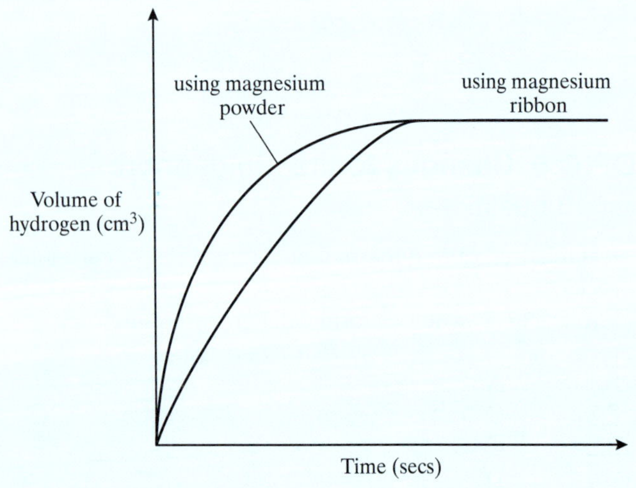

b) In a more concentrated acid there will be more particles of acid in a given volume and therefore more collisions will take place between particles of acid and particles of magnesium in a given time.

c) magnesium + hydrochloric acid
→ magnesium chloride + hydrogen **6**

> ***Examiner's Tip*** ✓
> *Take care with the drawing of sketch graphs like this one. The line will be a similar curve which is initially steeper, but which levels out quickly.*

2 a) The rate of carbon dioxide production decreases as the reaction proceeds. This is because as the acid get used up, its concentration decreases and there are fewer collisions per second between the acid and the calcium carbonate. The graph levels off at 83 cm^3 when all the acid has been used up and no more gas can be produced.

b) The new curve will be steeper initially and will level off at the same point (volume of carbon dioxide)

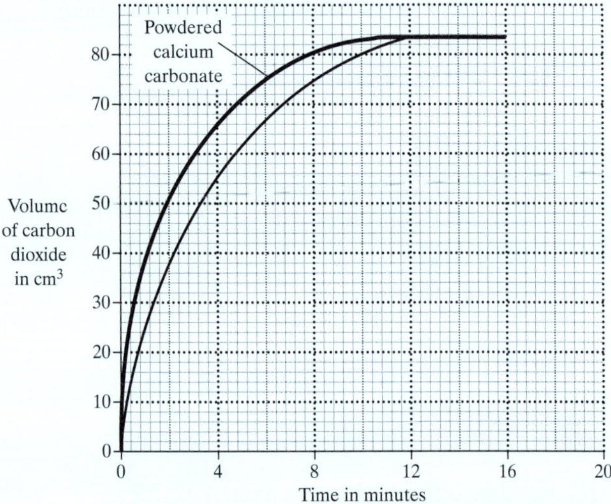

c) Changing the temperature, using an acid of different concentration and using a catalyst, will all change the rate of the reaction. (Any one of these suggestions will get the mark) **5**

> ***Examiner's Tip*** ✓
> *Take care to read the details with questions like this as changes in quantities will affect the shape of the graph produced.*
> *In this case the same amounts are used in both cases but powder is used instead of lumps in the second case. This means that in both cases the same final volume of carbon dioxide is produced.*

TOPIC 9. Enzymes

Year 11 questions

1 a) In beer making yeast converts ***sugar*** into carbon dioxide and ***alcohol***.
In yoghurt- making, bacteria convert ***milk sugar*** into ***lactic acid***.

b) The gas is bubbled through limewater. If the limewater becomes cloudy (ie a white precipitiate forms), the gas is carbon dioxide. **6**

Examiner's Tip ✓
When describing a test for a particular gas, be sure to include a description of a positive result to the test.

2 a) Alcohol produced in this way is used in making ***wine***
Carbon dioxide produced by fermentation can be used to make ***bread*** rise

b) i Enzymes work best at normal temperatures (around body temperature), so heating is not usually required.

ii If the temperature is increased, the enzyme can be easily damaged and become ineffective. **4**

3 a) 1. Barley
2. Water
3. Hops
4. Sugar
5. Maize
any four of these five will get 2 marks
any three of these five will get 1 mark

b) The enzyme will speed up the reaction without becoming used up in it.

c) Carbon dioxide gas

d) i Exothermic

ii If the solution becomes too hot, the enzyme will be denatured and will therefore become ineffective. **9**

Examiner's Tip ✓
In d) part ii be careful to avoid expressions like 'killing' – enzymes are not living and cannot therefore be killed. Heating affects the shape of the enzyme molecules and makes them ineffective.

TOPIC 10. Energy transfer
Year 11 questions

1 Exothermic
Released as heat **2**

2 a) Energy associated with bonds broken:
= (1 × H—H) + (1 × Cl—Cl) = 436 + 240 = 676
Energy associated with new bonds formed:
= 2 × H—Cl = 2 × 431 = 862
Energy exchanged with the surroundings
= 676 − 862 = −186 kJ mol^{-1}

Examiner's Tip ✓
The energy released by the formation of new bonds is greater than the energy required to break the bond in the reactant molecules and therefore the reaction is exothermic

b)

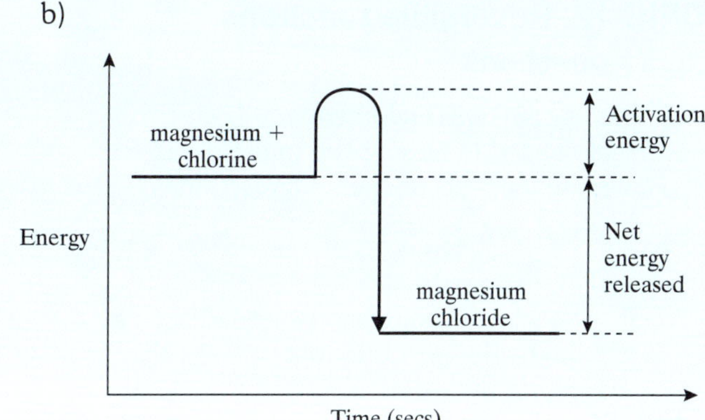

Examiner's Tip ✓
Note that the activation energy needs to be supplied in order to start the reaction. In this case, the energy of the reactants is higher than the energy of the products and thus the reaction is exothermic.

c) Endothermic

d) 125 $kJmol^{-1}$ taken in. **9**

TOPIC 11. Useful products from air
Year 11 questions

1 a) Air

b) i Platinum

ii Oxidation

c) i nitric acid + **potassium hydroxide**
→ potassium nitrate + **water**

ii Fertiliser

iii H^+ **7**

2 a) Iron is used as a catalyst to speed up the reaction

b) nitrogen + hydrogen ⇌ ammonia

c) i The reaction is reversible and so some of the ammonia which forms splits up to make nitrogen and hydrogen again.

ii The mixture of ammonia, nitrogen and hydrogen is cooled. This causes the ammonia gas to liquefy and separate from the unreacted hydrogen and nitrogen gases.

d) i Air

ii Hydrogen **7**

Examiner's Tip ✓
Note that in questions like this the information given on the diagram shown in the stem of the question can be of great help in answering questions about the process. A 'clue' is often given in the question.

TOPIC 12. Reversible reactions

Year 11 questions

1 a) The reaction was endothermic.
Heat needed to be supplied to the reactant in order to cause the reaction and to break bonds.

b) i The symbol $\rightleftarrows$ is used to indicate a reversible reaction

ii The white powder can be turned back to blue by adding water to it **3**

> ***Examiner's Tip*** ✓
> *The double (half) headed arrow is used to indicate a reaction which is a dynamic equilibrium.* $\rightleftharpoons$

2 a) The two half headed arrows: $\rightleftharpoons$ are used to represent a dynamic equilibrium

b) The value for ΔH is negative, thus the reaction is exothermic

c) i An increase in pressure favours the side of the reaction with fewer molecules so the equilibrium will move to the right.

ii Since the equilibrium moves to the right, the yield of ammonia will increase.

iii Since the forward reaction is exothermic, the reverse reaction is endothermic. An increase in temperature will therefore favour the reverse reaction, shifting the equilibrium to the left. This will reduce the yield of ammonia.

d) A relatively high temperature is needed in order to achieve an acceptable rate of reaction despite the fact that this reduces the yield.

e) A catalyst will speed up the rate of reaction without becoming used up itself. It will be more effective when finely divided as this increases its surface area. **10**

> ***Examiner's Tip*** ✓
> *It is important to note the economic importance of achieving an acceptable rate for industrial processes. The use of a catalyst allows industrial processes to be carried out at a cost effective rate but at lower (and therefore less costly) temperatures.*
> *Remember that a catalyst itself does not affect the position of equilibrium so does not change the percentage yield of product in a reversible reaction.*

TOPIC 13. Chemical calculations

Year 11 questions

1 a) Fe_2O_3 – Formula mass = (56 × 2) + (16 × 3)
= 112 + 48 = 160

b) % iron = (112/ 160) × 100 = 70%

c) Mass of iron in 1000 kg of iron oxide
= 1000 × (70/100) = 700 kg **6**

> ***Examiner's Tip*** ✓
> *Be sure to show all your working out in calculations like these.*

2 a) $CuFeS_2$ – Formula mass = 64 + 56 + (32 × 2)
= 184

b) % by mass of copper in copper pyrites

$$= \left(\frac{64}{184}\right) \times 100$$

= 34.8 % **3**

3 Fomula masses:

$\mathbf{H_2SO_4}$ = (2 × 1) + 32 + (4 × 16) = 98

$\mathbf{CaCO_3}$ = 40 + 12 + (3 × 16) = 100

From the equation sulphuric acid reacts with calcium carbonate in a ratio of 1:1

Therefore 98 g of sulphuric acid is neutralised by 100 g calcium carbonate

98 tonnes of sulphuric acid is neutralised by 100 tonnes calcium carbonate

1 tonne of sulphuric acid is neutralised by $\frac{100}{98}$ tonnes calcium carbonate

4600 tonne of sulphuric acid is neutralised by

$\left(\frac{100}{98}\right) \times 4600$ = 5000 tonnes calcium carbonate **3**

> ***Examiner's Tip*** ✓
> *This sort of calculation can be set out in different ways and still be correct. Note that you should show a series of logical steps in order to get full marks.*

4

	nitrogen	**oxygen**
mass /g	0.56	0.32
no. moles	0.56/14	0.32/16
	0.040	0.020

Ratio of moles 2 : 1

Therefore the formula of the nitrogen oxide is N_2O **4**

> ***Examiner's Tip*** ✓
> *It is very important in this type of question to set out your workings with care. A simple table like that used above is often helpful.*

TOPIC 14. Atomic structure

Year 11 questions

1 a) A = electron, B = neutron, C = proton
b) B
c) i 3 ii 3+ iii 27 **7**

2 a) 15
b) 16
c) 15 **3**

3 a) i

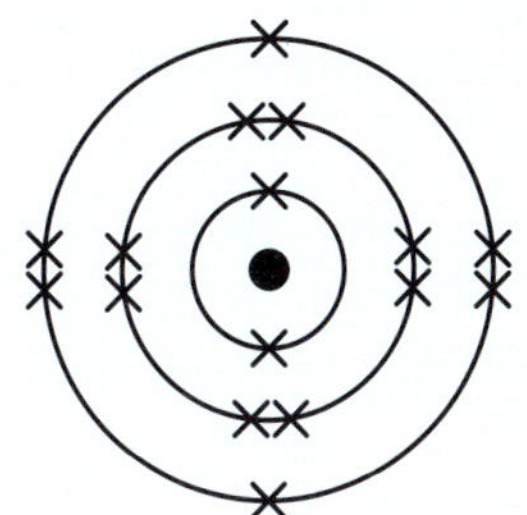

ii 32
iii S
b) Neutron **4**

TOPIC 15. Bonding

1 a) X is an ion ('atom' is acceptable)
Y is an electron
b) The atoms in metals are organised in a regular fashion in layers. Because of this, layers can, when subjected to external forces, slip easily over one another, allowing the metal to bend.
c) The atoms (or ions) are bonded together by a 'sea' of free electrons. The free electrons can drift through the metal (giant lattice) when a voltage is applied. **6**

Examiner's Tip ✓
The idea of a regular arrangement of atoms in a giant metallic lattice is important as it helps to explain many of the properties of metals.

2 a) $2\,Mg + O_2 \longrightarrow 2\,MgO$
b) i

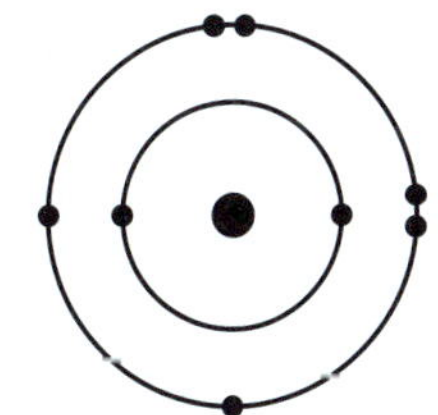

ii

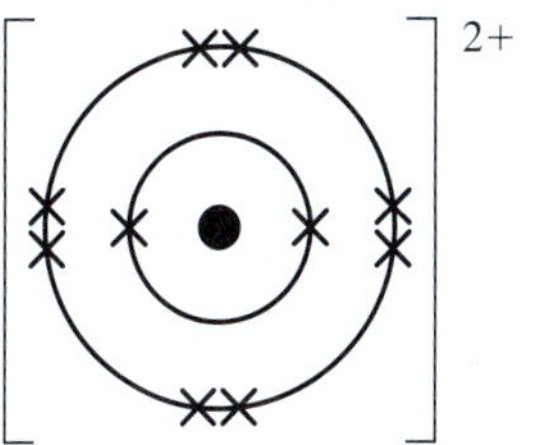

c) Ionic substances are made up of oppositely charged ions which attract one another in order to form an interlocking giant lattice. A lot of energy is needed to break up such a lattice and therefore it has a high melting point.
d) On descending the group, the atom of each successive element has an additional electron shell. This results in the electrons in the outermost shells becoming further from the nucleus and therefore more easily removed. Since metals react by losing their outer electrons, the elements lower down the group react more vigorously. **9**

Examiner's Tip ✓
This change in the number of electron shells is also the reason the reason the reactivity of the halogens decreases down the group. It gets more difficult for the halogen atoms to attract an extra electron into their outer shell the further it is from the attractive force of the nucleus.

TOPIC 16. The Periodic Table

1 a) i Y
ii W
iii X
iv Z
b) Group 7, the Halogens, and Group 0 the Noble gases **5**

Examiner's Tip ✓
With the exception of group 0 and the transition metals, the number of electrons in the outer shell of an atom gives the group number to which that element belongs.

2 a) The atomic number of the element
b) In the modern periodic table the vertical columns contain elements with similar electronic structures which therefore have similar properties to one another. This is more useful as it enables predictions about an element's behaviour to be made.
i Ca
ii Ne
iii Cs
iv P
v Am, Fm, Ha **7**

Examiner's Tip ✓
The modern periodic table is very helpful in enabling predictions about element's behaviour to be made. Remember the modern periodic table was constructed with gaps in it for those elements which had yet to be discovered.

TOPIC 17. Metal halides

Year 11 questions

1 a) i The chlorine bleaches the damp litmus paper, turning it white

ii Place a lighted splint at the mouth of the tube. If the gas burns with a squeaky pop, it is hydrogen

b i chlorine + sodium bromide $\rightarrow$ sodium chloride + bromine

ii This reaction shows that chlorine is more reactive than bromine since the chlorine oxidises bromide ions to bromine molecules/chlorine can displace bromide ions from solution, forming chloride ions. **5**

> **Examiner's Tip ✓**
> *Remember oxidation is the loss of electrons and reduction is the gaining of electrons. In this case the bromide is oxidised to bromine whilst the chlorine is reduced to chloride ions.*

2 a)

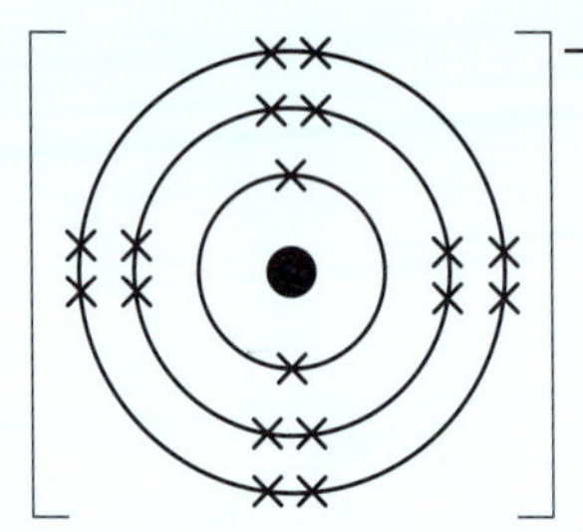

b) (l) is used to indicate that the substance is a liquid (aq) indicated that the substance is in aqueous solution (dissolved in water)

c) i $Cl_2(aq) + \mathbf{2}KBr(aq) \rightarrow \mathbf{2}KCl(aq) + Br_2(aq)$

ii Chlorine is more reactive than bromine and therefore will displace it. **6**

> **Examiner's Tip ✓**
> *The chorine is a more powerful oxidising agent and will therefore oxidise bromide to bromine.*

3 a) Metallic silver is produced

b) silver chloride (+ light) $\rightarrow$ silver metal + chlorine

c) Photochemical decomposition **4**

> **Examiner's Tip ✓**
> *This reaction explains why compounds of silver are used in conventional (non digital) photographic paper and films.*

TOPIC 18. Representing reactions

Year 11 question

1 a) i lead oxide + carbon $\rightarrow$ carbon dioxide + lead

ii

Substance	**mass/g**
Lead oxide	*446*
Carbon	*12*

Substance	**mass/g**
Lead	*414*
Carbon dioxide	***44 g***

> **Examiner's Tip ✓**
> *Note that mass is conserved. The total mass after reaction is equal to the total mass before reaction.*

b) i carbon dioxide + carbon $\rightarrow$ carbon monoxide

ii $C(s) + O_2(g) \rightarrow CO_2(g)$

iii $Fe_2O_3(s) + \mathbf{3}CO(g) \rightarrow \mathbf{2}Fe(l) + \mathbf{3}CO_2(g)$ **7**

> **Examiner's Tip ✓**
> *Note that each carbon monoxide combines with one oxygen. Thus in order to remove 3 oxygens from the iron, 3 carbon monoxides are required.*

2 a) i copper chloride $\rightarrow$ copper + chlorine

ii $Cu^{2+}(aq) + 2e^- \rightarrow Cu\,(s)$

iii $\mathbf{2}Cl^-(aq) \rightarrow Cl_2 + \mathbf{2}e^-(g)$ **5**

> **Examiner's Tip ✓**
> *Remember: **O**xidation **is** **l**oss, **r**eduction **is** **g**ain*
>
> *and*
>
> *Redu**C**tion takes place at the **C**athode, oxid**a**tion at the **a**node*

TOPIC 19. Aqueous chemistry

1 Solubility curves

a) The solubility of these salts increases as the temperature increases

b) Temperature has a large effect on the solubility of potassium nitrate. The solubility of sodium chloride is only slightly affected by a change in temperature.

c) i 35 g ± 1 g

ii 57°C ± 2°C

iii potassium nitrate (white) crystals would appear **6**

2 Acids and water

a) The magnesium reacts more vigorously in the hydrochloric acid

b) The hydrochloric acid is the more reactive of the two acids

c) The hydrochloric acid is a strong acid – this means that all its molecules had ionised to form hydrogen ions. The ethanoic acid is not fully ionised – its molecules are in dynamic equilibrium with its ions. **4**

3 Hard water

a) Water which has either calcium or ***magnesium*** ions dissolved in it is described as hard water. This can form when a river flows over an area where the rock type is gypsum (which is calcium sulphate). This compound is slightly ***soluble*** in water and so the ***calcium*** ions get into the water. Limestone (which is mainly ***calcium carbonate***) is not soluble in water but will dissolve due to the action of ***carbonic acid***, formed when carbon dioxide in the atmosphere is dissolved in rainwater.

b) Limescale can clog up pipes and heating elements. Hard water will react with soap to produce a scum, making it more difficult to get a lather.

c) i Temporary hardness is hardness which can be removed by boiling
   ii Permanent hardness is hardness which remains even after the water has been boiled

d) *Either:* The water can be passed through an ion exchange resin which exchanges calcium ions for sodium ions.
   or: Washing soda (sodium carbonate) is added to the water to precipitate out the calcium ions as calcium carbonate. **11**

TOPIC 20. Forming salts

1 Soluble salts

a) $HCl(aq) + NaOH(aq) \longrightarrow NaCl(aq) + H_2O(l)$

b) A small volume of sodium hydroxide solution had a few drops of universal indicator solution added to it. Hydrochloric acid was added little by little, with stirring until the indicator is a green (neutral) colour.

c) The charcoal is used to absorb the colour from the indicator

d) Heating evaporates water from the solution so that crystals will form on cooling

e) i Acid reacts with the alkali in a ratio of 1:1. Since the concentration of the hydroxide is half that of the acid, then twice the volume will be need to neutralise it. Thus $10 \times 2 =$ **20 cm³** sodium hydroxide will be needed.
   ii No of moles of sodium chloride produced = no of moles of acid used

$$\frac{\text{molarity} \times \text{volume}}{1000} = \frac{0.1 \times 10}{1000} = \mathbf{0.001\ moles}$$

   iii formula mass of sodium chloride $= 23 + 35.5 = 58.5$
   mass = formula mass × no of moles
   $= 0.001 \times 58.5 = \mathbf{0.0585\ g}$ **10**

Examiner's Tip ✓
It is possible to carry out this type of preparation by performing it twice – once as a titration with the indicator to find the volume required, and a second time without the indicator. This avoids using the indicator and charcoal, and there will be no need to filter.

2 Insoluble salts

You will find the table of formulae of some common ions helpful in answering this question.

a) reaction 2 – barium sulphate
   reaction 3 – lead iodide

b) $Na_2SO_4(aq) + BaCl_2(aq) \longrightarrow 2NaCl(aq) + BaSO_4(s)$
   $2NaI(aq) + Pb(NO_3)_2(aq) \longrightarrow 2NaNO_3(aq) + PbI_2(s)$

c) The solutions are mixed then filtered. The precipitate retained on the filter paper is then washed with distilled water before being scraped onto fresh filter paper and allowed to dry. **9**

Examiner's Tip ✓
Precipitates will need careful washing with distilled water and drying in order to obtain pure samples of these salts.

3 Insoluble base + Acid

a) $CuO(s) + H_2SO_4(aq) \longrightarrow CuSO_4(aq) + H_2O(l)$

b) Step 1 Copper oxide is added one spatula measure at a time, with stirring, to sulphuric acid in a beaker. This reacts to produce copper sulphate solution. Copper oxide is added until it is in excess
   Step 2 The solution resulting from step 1 is filtered to remove excess copper oxide, leaving a pure solution of copper sulphate
   Step 3 The solution is heated to evaporate some of the water to help it to crystallise on cooling **4**

Examiner's Tip ✓
It is important to ensure that the solid is in excess in step 1. You can warm the reacting mixture gently at this point. This ensures that the acid is neutralised completely.

TOPIC 21. Organic chemistry

1 Alcohols

a) i Carbon dioxide
   ii glucose $\xrightarrow{\text{yeast}}$ ethanol + carbon dioxide

b) $C_2H_4(g) + H_2O(g) \longrightarrow C_2H_5OH(l)$ or (g)

c) i The process involving ethene can be a continuous process
   ii The fermentation process uses a renewable resource.

d) Ethanol can be used as a fuel and as a solvent **8**

Examiner's Tip ✓
The use of ethanol as a fuel has a number of environmental advantages. Ethanol burns with a clean flame and if made from sugar, it makes no overall contribution to global warming.

2 Isomers

a) i Isomer A will have the higher boiling point
   ii The straight chain alkane molecules can pack together better and therefore will have stronger forces between the molecules than those of the branched chain alkane.

b) There will be no chemical differences between these two isomers, since they have the same atoms and types of bonds as each other. **5**

Examiner's Tip ✓
Not all isomers will have identical chemical properties – but provided the two isomer have the same functional groups then it is likely they will undergo the same reactions (perhaps at a different rate).

3 Carboxylic acids

a) Ethanoic acid CH_3COOH
Propanoic acid C_2H_5COOH

b) i The magnesium will dissolve, giving off hydrogen gas, forming a solution of the magnesium (carboxylate) salt

ii The sodium carbonate solution will effervesce, giving off carbon dioxide gas and a solution of the sodium (carboxylate) salt of the acid.

c) i Esters

ii alcohols + carboxylic acids → ester + water

d) Esters are used in flavourings and perfumes. **10**

Examiner's Tip ✓
Note that although carboxylic acids show many of the chemical properties of acids, they are only partly ionised and thus behave as weak acids.

TOPIC 22. Industrial processes

1 Sulphuric acid

a) sulphur + oxygen → sulphur dioxide

b) i $2SO_2(g) + O_2(g) \rightleftharpoons 2SO_3$

ii The reaction is in a state of dynamic equilibrium

c) $SO_3(g) + H_2O(l) \rightarrow H_2SO_4(l)$

d) Detergents, fertilisers, car batteries, as a dehydrating agent (any two) **9**

Examiner's Tip ✓
The third stage actually involves the addition of sulphur trioxide to sulphuric acid. This avoids the formation of a thick mist of sulphuric acid.

2 Extracting titanium

a) It is used for making strong and corrosion resistant alloys

b) Titanium dioxide is separated from the ore called ilmenite which also contains iron oxide using magnets. The TiO_2 is heated with ***carbon*** and ***chlorine***. This produces titanium chloride and carbon dioxide gas. The products are then ***cooled*** and the titanium chloride condenses to a liquid. This liquid is purified by ***distillation***. The titanium chloride is the ***reduced*** by sodium metal in an atmosphere of argon.

c) i $TiCl_4(g) + 4Na(l) \rightarrow Ti(s) + 4NaCl(l)$

ii The titanium is ***Red***uced (gains electrons); the sodium is **ox**idised (loses electrons). Hence reduction and oxidation take place simultaneously **8**

Examiner's Tip ✓
Although there is no oxygen involved this is still a redox reaction. Remember oxidation is the loss of electrons, reduction is the gain of electrons.

3 Making steel

a) i It combines with the carbon to form carbon dioxide gas which is given off.

ii $C(s) + O_2(g) \rightarrow CO_2(g)$

b) i A mixture of two or more metals

ii The mixing of metals changes the way in which the atoms in the metal behave and can give the alloy useful properties such as corrosion resistance and high strength. **6**

Examiner's Tip ✓
Lime is used to combine with any acidic oxides formed in the steel-making process and forms a slag which floats on the surface and can be skimmed off.

TOPIC 23. Detection and identification

Precipitation reactions

1 a) An insoluble solid formed as the result of a reaction taking place in solution.

b) i silver nitrate + sodium chloride
→ silver chloride + sodium nitrate

ii Silver chloride

iii Chloride ions

c) i Dip a loop of clean wire into pure water then into a sample of the solid to be tested. Put the wire and sample at the tip of the blue cone of a Bunsen Burner flame with the air hole open. Note the colour of the flame produced.

ii Bright yellow. **9**

Unknown compound

2 a) Potassium / K^+

b) Sulphate / SO_4^{2-}

c) K_2SO_4

d) $K_2SO_4(aq) + BaCl_2(aq)$
$\rightarrow BaSO_4(s) + 2KCl(aq)$ **5**

Identification

3 a) *Reaction 1.* When a sample of copper carbonate was heated in a test tube, its colour changed from a ***green*** powder to copper oxide which is a ***black*** powder. Carbon dioxide gas was given off in this process. This gas was identified by the fact that it produced a ***white*** precipitate when bubbled through limewater.
Reaction 2. When dilute acid was added to a sample of the copper carbonate, bubbles of ***colourless*** gas were produced.
Reaction 3. The copper oxide produced in 1 was added to dilute nitric acid until no more would dissolve. Excess copper oxide was then filtered out. The resultant solution was tested by the addition of sodium hydroxide solution. This reacted with the metal ions present, to produce a ***pale blue*** precipitate

b) Copper carbonate → copper oxide + carbon dioxide
Thermal decomposition

c) Green powder dissolved in colourless liquid to produce bubbles of colourless gas and producing a blue/green solution.

d) i Neutralisation

ii $CuO(s) + 2HNO_3(aq)$
$\rightarrow Cu(NO_3)_2(aq) + H_2O(l)$ **10**

Data Sheet

1 Reactivity Series of Metals

Potassium	most reactive ↑
Sodium	
Calcium	
Magnesium	
Aluminium	
Carbon	
Zinc	
Iron	
Tin	
Lead	
Hydrogen	
Copper	
Silver	
Gold	
Platinum	↓ least reactive

(elements in italics, though non-metals, have been included for comparison).

---

2 Formulae of Some Common Ions

Positive ions

Name	Formula
Hydrogen	H^+
Sodium	Na^+
Silver	Ag^+
Potassium	K^+
Lithium	Li^+
Ammonium	NH_4^+
Barium	Ba^{2+}
Calcium	Ca^{2+}
Copper(II)	Cu^{2+}
Magnesium	Mg^{2+}
Zinc	Zn^{2+}
Lead	Pb^{2+}
Iron(II)	Fe^{2+}
Iron(III)	Fe^{3+}
Aluminium	Al^{3+}

Negative ions

Name	Formula
Chloride	Cl^-
Bromide	Br^-
Fluoride	F^-
Iodide	I^-
Hydroxide	OH^-
Nitrate	NO_3^-
Oxide	O^{2-}
Sulphide	S^{2-}
Sulphate	SO_4^{2-}
Carbonate	CO_3^{2-}

KEY

Relative atomic mass A_r Atomic number (Proton number) Z	1 **H** Hydrogen 1

1	2											3	4	5	6	7	0
																	4 **He** Helium 2
7 **Li** Lithium 3	9 **Be** Beryllium 4											11 **B** Boron 5	12 **C** Carbon 6	14 **N** Nitrogen 7	16 **O** Oxygen 8	19 **F** Fluorine 9	20 **Ne** Neon 10
23 **Na** Sodium 11	24 **Mg** Magnesium 12											27 **Al** Aluminium 13	28 **Si** Silicon 14	31 **P** Phosphorus 15	32 **S** Sulphur 16	35.5 **Cl** Chlorine 17	40 **Ar** Argon 18
39 **K** Potassium 19	40 **Ca** Calcium 20	45 **Sc** Scandium 21	48 **Ti** Titanium 22	51 **V** Vanadium 23	52 **Cr** Chromium 24	55 **Mn** Manganese 25	56 **Fe** Iron 26	59 **Co** Cobalt 27	59 **Ni** Nickel 28	64 **Cu** Copper 29	65 **Zn** Zinc 30	70 **Ga** Gallium 31	73 **Ge** Germanium 32	75 **As** Arsenic 33	79 **Se** Selenium 34	80 **Br** Bromine 35	84 **Kr** Krypton 36
85 **Rb** Rubidium 37	88 **Sr** Strontium 38	89 **Y** Yttrium 39	91 **Zr** Zirconium 40	93 **Nb** Niobium 41	96 **Mo** Molybdenum 42	99 **Tc** Technetium 43	101 **Ru** Ruthenium 44	103 **Rh** Rhodium 45	106 **Pd** Palladium 46	108 **Ag** Silver 47	112 **Cd** Cadmium 48	115 **In** Indium 49	119 **Sn** Tin 50	122 **Sb** Antimony 51	128 **Te** Tellurium 52	127 **I** Iodine 53	131 **Xe** Xenon 54
133 **Cs** Caesium 55	137 **Ba** Barium 56	139 **La** Lanthanum 57	178 **Hf** Hafnium 72	181 **Ta** Tantalum 73	184 **W** Tungsten 74	186 **Re** Rhenium 75	190 **Os** Osmium 76	192 **Ir** Iridium 77	195 **Pt** Platinum 78	197 **Au** Gold 79	201 **Hg** Mercury 80	204 **Tl** Thallium 81	207 **Pb** Lead 82	209 **Bi** Bismuth 83	**Po** Polonium 84	**At** Astatine 85	**Rn** Radon 86
Fr Francium 87	226 **Ra** Radium 88	227 **Ac** Actinium 89															

Elements 58-71 and 90-103 have been omitted.

Index

Published in 2005 by:
Nelson Thornes Ltd
Delta Place
27 Bath Road
CHELTENHAM
GL53 7TH
United Kingdom

05 06 07 08 09 / 10 9 8 7 6 5 4 3 2 1

A catalogue record for this book is available from the British Library

ISBN 0 7487 9586 3

Page make-up by Tech-Set
Printed in Croatia by Zrinski

Acknowledgements

We would like to thank examiners Bob McDuell and David Fowkes for their help with the examination questions, answers and tips.

AQA acknowledgements

AQA examination questions are reproduced by permission of the Assessment and Qualifications Alliance.

Chap. 1 Double Award Modular/Science:Chemistry (Modular) – Metals Module 5 – Foundation Tier March 2003 Q1; Double Award Modular/Science:Chemistry (Modular) – Metals Module 5 – Foundation Tier March 2003 Q2; Double Award Modular/Science:Chemistry (Modular) – Metals Module 5 – Foundation Tier March 2003 Q6; Double Award Modular/Science:Chemistry (Modular) – Metals Module 5 – Foundation Tier March 2003 Q8; Science: Double Award (Modular) Higher Tier – Paper 1 June 2003 Q4; Chap. 2 Double Award Modular/Science:Chemistry (Modular) – Metals Module 5 – Foundation Tier March 2003 Q3; Double Award Modular/Science:Chemistry (Modular) – Metals Module 5 – Foundation Tier March 2003 Q5; Science: Double Award (Modular) Higher Tier – Paper 2 June 03 Q11; Science: Double Award (Modular) Higher Tier – Paper 1 June 03 Q12; Chap. 3 Double Award Modular/Science:Chemistry (Modular) – Metals Module 5 – Foundation Tier March 2003 Q7; Double Award Modular/Science:Chemistry (Modular) – Metals Module 5 – Higher Tier March 2003 Q9; Science: Single Award (Modular) – Foundation Tier June 2001 Q20; Chap. 4 Science: Double Award (Modular) Science: Chemistry (modular) – Earth materials (module 06) – Foundation Tier March 2003 Q8; Science: Double Award (modular)/Science: Chemistry (modular) – Earth materials (module 06) – Foundation June 2003 Q4; Chap. 5 Science: Double Award (Modular)/Science: Chemistry (Modular) – Earth materials (module 06) – Foundation Tier March 2003 Q4; Science: Double Award (Modular)/Science: Chemistry (Modular) – Earth materials (module 06) – Foundation Tier March 2003 Q9; Science: Double Award (Modular) – Higher Tier – Paper 2 9 June 2003 Q14; Chap. 6 Science: Double Award (modular)/Science: Chemistry (modular) – Earth materials (module 06) – Higher Tier March 2003 Q4; Science: Double Award (modular)/Science: Chemistry (modular) – Earth materials (module 06) – Foundation Tier 24 June 2003 Q10; Science: Double Award (modular)/Science: Chemistry (modular) – Earth materials (module 06) – Foundation Tier March 2003 Q1; Chap. 7 Science: Double Award (modular)/Science: Chemistry (modular) – Earth materials (module 06) – Foundation June 2003 Q3; Science: Double Award (modular)/Science: Chemistry (modular) – Earth materials (module 06) – Higher Tier June 2003 Q9; Science: Double Award (modular)/Science: Chemistry (modular) – Earth materials (module 06) – Foundation Tier March 2003 Q2; Chap. 8 Science: Single Award (modular) – Higher Tier June 2001 Q9; Science: Double Award (modular) – Higher Tier – Paper 2 June 2003 Q4; Chap. 9 Science: Single Award (modular) Foundation Tier June 2003 Q4; Science: Double Award (modular) – Foundation Tier – Paper 2 June 2003 Q6; Science: Double Award(co-ordinated) Foundation Tier – Paper 2 June 2001 Q15; Chap. 10 Paper 2421 Science: Single Award (Modular) – Foundation Tier June 2001 Q7; Science: Single Award (Modular) June 2001 10; Science: Double Award (Modular) June 2003 Q10; Chap. 11 Science: Single Award (co-ordinated) – Foundation Tier June 2003 Q3; Science: Double Award (Modular) – Foundation Tier – Paper 2 9 June 2003 Q16; Chap. 12 Science: Double Award (co-ordinated) – Foundation Tier June 2003 Q9; Chap. 13 Science: Double Award (co-ordinated) – Foundation Tier June 2003 15 cScience: Double Award (co-ordinated) 11 June 2001 13 e; Science: Double Award (co-ordinated) paper 2 – Higher Tier 11 June 2001 6 c; Science: Double Award (co-ordinated) Paper 2 – Higher Tier 11 June 2001 7 c ; Chap. 14 Science: Double Award (co-ordinated) Paper 2 – Foundation Tier June 2001 Q2; Science: Single Award (co-ordinated) Paper 2 – Higher Tier 11 June 2001 Q6; Chap. 15 Science: Double Award (Modular) – Higher Tier Paper 1 2 June 2003 Q15; Science: Double Award (co-ordinated) Paper 2 – Higher Tier June 2001 Q9
Chap. 16 Science: Double Award (Modular) – Higher Tier Paper 1 June 2003 Q4; Science: Double Award – (Co-ordinated) Paper 2 – Higher Tier 11 June 2001 Q3; Chap. 17 Science: Single Award (Modular) – Higher Tier 5 June 2001 Q8; Science: Double Award (Modular) – Higher Tier – Paper 1 June 2003 Q5

Please note that the following AQA(NEAB) questions used on pages 19, 42, 47, 50, 51, 62, 63, 68, 69, 73, 76–77, 80 are NOT from the live examinations for the current specification.

AQA take no responsibility for answers given to their questions within this publication.

Photograph acknowledgements

Photodisc 18 (NT), p.78.